D1050730

THE JOY OF VISUALIZATION

75 Creative Ways to Improve Your Life

by
Valerie Wells

CHRONICLE BOOKS
SAN FRANCISCO

Copyright © 1990 by Valerie Wells. All rights reserved.
No part of this book may be reproduced in any form without
written permission from the publisher.

Printed in the United States

Library of Congress Cataloging in Publication Data
Wells, Valerie.
The joy of visualization : seventy-five creative ways to improve your
life / by Valerie Wells.
p.   cm.
ISBN 0-87701-765-4
1. Success—Psychological aspects.   2. Visualization—Problems,
exercises, etc.   I. Title.
BF637.S8W365   1990
153.3'2—dc20   90-37216
CIP

Cover Design: John Miller
Book Design: Words & Deeds, Inc.

Distributed in Canada by Raincoast Books
112 East Third Avenue, Vancouver, B.C. V5T 1C8

10 9 8 7 6 5 4 3

Chronicle Books
275 Fifth Street
San Francisco, California
94103

ACKNOWLEDGMENTS

▼

The following people came into my life as the result of visualizing what I wanted. Some inspired visualizations. Some inspired me by believing in me and providing insight and laughter. Some provided emotional and/or financial support. Without them this book might never have been conceived, and certainly would not have been born.

I especially thank my agent, Heide Lange, for her unflagging confidence and persistence, and my editor, Nion McEvoy, for being able to visualize these visualizations as a book. And my heartfelt thanks to Concept: Synergy for helping to open my inner eyes and improving my inner vision.

For each of you I visualize joy and success abounding in your life. Visualize me singing you a merry song of thank you.

Christine Bell	Robin Loncaric
Joe Cafaro	Ruth Johnstone Lord
Bruce Caldwell	Larry Mark
Troy Campbell	Barbara McCrea
Michael Catanzaro	Mario Morin
Chi-Ling	Evan Rhodes
Flying Cloud	Bill Richardson
Richard Frankel	Roberta
Chris Gilson	John Rothchild
Carole Hall	Robert Sauve
Kathy Higgins	Joseph Shorr
Kathy Hersh	Peter Skolnik
Laura Kelly	Harry Sloan
Gertude Kraus	Ira Stein
Lazaris	Frank Thornton
Ling-Li	Roger Wisner

I also thank the owners and staffs of Market to Market, the Palace, and the News Cafe for allowing me to sit at their sunny tables for hours while I wrote.

CONTENTS
▼

PROBLEM SOLVING

MENTAL and EMOTIONAL HEALTH

PHYSICAL HEALTH

I: VISUALIZATION
WHAT IT IS AND WHAT IT DOES

What you think is what you get. That's the basic principle of visualization. The thoughts you generate inside your head have a powerful effect on your outer life, affecting success, relationships, career, wealth, health, and happiness. Negative thoughts have a negative effect, and positive thoughts have a positive effect.

The idea that your mental world has impact on your physical world isn't new. Over two thousand years ago, in 19 B.C., the poet Virgil wrote in the *Aeneid*, "Mind moves matter."

Today people from all walks of life are successfully using mind-over-matter visualization techniques for a variety of purposes. They create pictures in their minds of what they want, and get it! Athletes use it to win: diver Greg Louganis and skater Elizabeth Manley have publicly attributed their Olympic medals to visualization. Patients use visualization to conquer cancer, migraine headaches, high blood pressure, and obesity. Salespeople count on it to increase sales. People in high-tension jobs use it to reduce stress.

Using mind over matter works, and it means that your mind definitely matters. What you focus your mind on matters. What you feed your mind matters. The kinds of pictures you hold in your mind matter.

Keeping your mind in mind matters because the quality of your thoughts affects the quality of your life. This means that you can take charge of your life by taking charge of your thoughts, and you can take charge of your thoughts with the help of visualization. Visualization is simply the process of creating pictures in your mind, giving form to your thoughts so you can more easily direct them toward a specific goal. It is a way of achieving creative control over your life. By creating positive mental pictures of the kind of life you want to have, you significantly increase the possibility of having it. A Latin axiom states: *Fortis imaginatio generat causum* ("A strong imagination begets the event itself").

How do you see the pictures in your mind? With your mind's eye. But what if you think your mental eyesight is about as keen as a white goose's in a blizzard? Check to see if that's just a limiting belief you're holding onto. Maybe you didn't really know what visualization was, and so you decided you couldn't do it. Or you might have thought it was something highfalutin and complicated that you weren't capable of doing.

Try to suspend the belief that you can't visualize, because just about everybody has some degree of mental eyesight. How would you find your keys, or your car, or your way home without being able to conjure up a mental picture of what each looks like and where it's located?

True, just as the sharpness of people's physical eyesight varies, so does their mindsight. The mental picture you have of your front door, or a pink hippo in a tutu, might not be photo-clear. It could be fuzzy and out of focus, or long on outlines, short on details. You may have more of a *sense*, or a feeling, of it than an actual picture. What matters is that the image, or the "sense" of it, is recognizable. If you can picture—or sense—the bed you sleep in, or your best friend's face, be assured that you can visualize.

The more you visualize what you want in each area of your life, the more you receive what you want. And the more you visualize, the more you feel empowered. The very act of visualizing brings a sense of well-being, an increased sense of confidence, and a feeling of being in charge. Experiencing your ability to take effective action in your mental world—creating what you want and solving problems—is immensely satisfying. As the creative power of your mind increases, it spills over into other activities, giving you a joyful sense of being able to take effective action in your physical world.

With visualization it is definitely true that a picture is worth a thousand words. It can also be said that a visualization is worth a thousand efforts. That your thoughts have direct impact on your physical world was demonstrated by an experiment done in the 1930s. Two golfers with identical handicaps were given a month to practice and improve their game. One golfer practiced his swing on the golf course every day. The second golfer sat in an armchair every day for fifteen minutes, visualizing himself swinging his club smoothly, and "seeing" the ball arc gracefully down the fairway to land on the green. At the end of thirty days the two golfers played a round of golf together. Who won? The armchair visualizer who had practiced his swing in his mind; his score had improved significantly!

Visualization is fun, easy to do, and it works! To help yourself understand it—and warm your mind up for visualizing—consider these analogies:

Using visualization is just like using electricity: you don't have to know exactly how it works to use it effectively. With electricity you only need to know that electrical energy is available, have a use for it, and take appropriate action to switch it on. You can flip a switch and have light without knowing about electrons and Ohm's law.

The same is true for visualization. All you need to know is that visualization power is available, have a use for it, and take appropriate action to turn it on. You can switch on a visualization and enjoy the light of insight and success without knowing what synapses are taking place between which dendrites.

Visualization can also be thought of as a language that uses pictures instead of words. Your mind doesn't store experiences of the past and dreams for the future as words on paper, but as images and sense impressions. It translates those images into words that you can speak, but "picturese" is your mind's native language.

This pictorial language is especially useful for carrying on a conversation between your conscious and subconscious minds. Your subconscious is like a computer stored with data, and just as computers have a language, so does your subconscious; it "speaks" in pictures, and "hears" in pictures. Your subconscious mind has an extensive working vocabulary of mental pictures—some literal, some symbolic—with which to carry on a two-way conversation with your conscious mind. Visualization flips the switch that starts the conversation flowing.

Why do you want to talk to your subconscious? Because it contains valuable information about where you think you've been, who you think you are, and where you think you're going. The positive or negative pictures stored in your mind about your past and future have a powerful effect on your present. For instance, if you were chronically ill as a child, the experience of being sick could have caused you to store images of yourself as an unwell person. You then projected the images of being ill into the future, "seeing" yourself as a person who is often sick. The combination of past and future pictures of being sick can predispose you to being ill in the present.

The greater the number of negative (limiting or destructive) mental images you create and store, the more negative energy they generate. The more negative energy that's generated, the more your life will tend to be dominated by negative rather than positive circumstances.

Computer programmers have a saying: "Garbage in, garbage out." That means that if you put garbage information into a computer, garbage information is what you'll get out. Ditto for your subconscious. If you've stored negative images of pain, struggle, or disappointment in your subconscious, that's what you're apt to get in your day-to-day life, because your subconscious is running a program that says that pain, struggle, or disappointment is what is true for you. You get out what you put in.

The good news is that help, in the form of visualization, is here. By using the seventy-five creative visualizations in this book, you can talk directly with your subconscious, replacing limiting negative mental pictures with expansive positive ones. The more often you entertain positive thoughts, the more welcome they become, until they take up permanent residence, leaving little or no room for negative thoughts. When you erase "garbage" from the past and change your vision of the future, you successfully tell your subconscious computer how you want you and your life to look. The result? A better and brighter life. The present truly becomes a present: a gift from you to you to enjoy.

II: VISUALIZATION
HOW, WHY, WHEN, AND
WHERE TO USE IT

These seventy-five visualizations are fast, fun, and effective. In a world in which we are increasingly busy juggling careers, family, and personal life, these visualizations offer a quick, easy way to achieve creative control over your life. Each visualization offers insight and provides an imaginative course of action for change.

The visualizations are grouped into five categories: "Goal Getting," "Image Shining," "Problem Solving," "Mental and Emotional Health," and "Physical Health." There are several ways to choose a visualization. You can check the table of contents under the category that best fits your need that moment, and pick a title that appeals to you. Or pick several titles, reading through the visualizations until you find one that tickles your fancy.

Or maybe you feel that doing a visualization would be helpful, or even fun, but don't have a specific goal or need. If you want to be spontaneous, open the book at random and read whichever visualization the pages fall open to. Each visualization is just two pages long, arranged on the left- and right-hand pages, so you can turn to one visualization at a time. Or you can hold a particular section between thumb and forefinger, then let the pages fall open.

Once you've chosen a visualization, read it over a couple of times in order to become familiar with the concept and the sequence of images. Because you'll be reading the visualizations instead of listening to someone guide you through, don't expect to be lulled into a relaxed alpha state.

The visualizations are designed to be entertaining in order to grab the attention of both your conscious and subconscious mind, and to imprint positive images on both levels. Your subconscious enjoys having something unusual or unexpected happen within a familiar context.

Don't be afraid to make these visualizations your own. Adapt them to your particular needs and creative inclinations, but keep them simple. If you complicate the visualization, you'll give your subconscious the message that you want your life and your successes to be complicated.

Once you're able to remember the flow of images in a visualization, you can do it anywhere, anytime you have a couple of minutes: on waking or before going to sleep, in the shower, on a bus, jogging, during work breaks, while stopped at a red light, on hold on the telephone, bicycling, waiting in line, etc. After you become familiar with several visualizations, you'll have a colorful assortment in mind to choose from.

The more often you reinforce positive images, the better the results. You can read one visualization a day, or one a week, using that image as your positive focus for that period of time. These visualizations are fast and fun so that you can do them quickly, have a good time, and still benefit. In fact, the more fun you have, the better the results.

The more often you visualize, the more powerfully your conscious mind imprints the positive images on your subconscious, and the more you'll achieve your goals!

How do you visualize? This is one instance in which something is easier done than said. You don't need any special equipment to visualize, just three basic tools:

1. A mind.

2. A heart.

3. A will (as in "where there's a will, there's a way").

If you are able to add two plus two, feel glad to see a friend, and get yourself up in the morning, you already possess all three. Equipped with these three tools, you're ready to visualize.

THE FOUR STEPS OF VISUALIZATION

1. CHOOSE YOUR GOAL, using both your mind *and* your heart. It might be something you want to have. Or do. Or be. It might have to do with love, money, career, health, personal growth, fun, relationships, etc.

It's much easier to *get* what you want when you *know* what you want. Doing a visualization is like taking a picture with a camera. If you don't aim your camera at the subject you want a picture of, you could wind up with a photo of a passing garbage truck instead of what you wanted.

The tricky bit with this step is getting your mind and your heart to agree. Sometimes your mind thinks it wants something, but it's a "should" want. You want it because you think it's the proper thing to want, or because it's expected of you by someone else, but your heart isn't really in it. At other times your heart yearns for something, but your mind censors it as being unattainable, or censors you as being undeserving.

Being honest with yourself about what you want helps your mind and your heart to agree. When your mind and heart are in agreement about a goal, your will follows close behind. Willingness precedes and initiates taking action, such as doing a visualization. If you want to take a picture you must be willing to push the shutter button.

2. FOCUS THE PICTURE with your mind. Think of your conscious mind as the camera and your subconscious as the film. You need to form as clear a mental picture as possible in order for a sharp image to be imprinted on the film.

Being relaxed is important because it helps focus the picture more clearly. If you're tense, or have the jitters, the camera of your mind will shake and the image will be blurred. So, r-e-e-l-a-a-a-a-x. Stamp your feet a couple of times to ground yourself. Shake out tension through your hands. Take a slow, deep breath. Get mentally loose.

Let the visualization picture form in your mind, bringing it into sharp focus. Notice details. Enliven it with color. If you can't see it, sense it. Your eyes can be opened or closed, depending on what you're doing and where you are.

It is *very, very, very* important to see yourself in the visualization you've chosen. If you aren't in the picture, your subconscious won't know whom the picture is for, and it might develop the picture, but you won't be part of it. You might visualize a swimming pool brimming with money, but if you don't see *yourself* frolicking in that money-pool, it could be your pizza delivery man or your mother-in-law who enjoys a financial windfall.

3. FEEL THE EXPERIENCE of the visualization. You used your mind to *see* yourself in the picture, now use your heart to *feel* yourself in the picture. Participate in it with all your senses. Get right inside the image and experience it as if it were actually happening, feeling the excitement and joy of having what you want.

The fuller and richer your emotional experience, the better the visualization works, because it's the emotional exposure that illuminates the image and imprints it on the film of your subconscious. Positive emotions create an electric flash of light that helps bring the image to life.

4. ALLOW THE VISUALIZATION TO SUCCEED. Consciously giving yourself permission for the visualization to work is like developing the film. If you don't believe that the visualization will work, or if you have a negative attitude about it, the picture won't develop properly, if at all.

Believe that the visualization will work, as strongly as you believe that the sun will come up in the morning. Believe in it just as you believe that electricity brings light, that speaking a common language facilitates communication, that a computer stores data, and that a camera takes pictures. Trust in your ability to visualize, and in the power of visualization.

When you have used your mind and your heart to know what you want, have been willing to take visualization action, have formed a mental picture of your goal, and have experienced the excitement of having it, you're ready to pick up your photos.

Visualization power is available, you have a use for it, and you know how to switch it on.

Get the picture?

THE FOUR STEPS OF VISUALIZATION

1. CHOOSE YOUR GOAL.
2. FOCUS THE PICTURE.
3. FEEL THE EXPERIENCE.
4. ALLOW THE VISUALIZATION TO SUCCEED.

VISUALIZATIONS

▼

▼

▼

▼

Fortis Imaginatio Generat Causum

"A strong imagination begets the event itself"

GOAL GETTING

I

SUCCESS SHIP

Have you been waiting for your ship to come in, but can't even see a dot on the horizon? Or did your ship come in, but it turned out to be a dinghy? Use the following visualization to increase your capacity for success.

Imagine that you're standing at the end of a dock. A breeze tousles your hair. Water slaps against the pilings. Seagulls wheel overhead. Sea and sky stretch before you, clear and blue.

As you scan the horizon for your ship, think about success. What kinds of success do you want? Career? Love? Financial? Health? Relationships? Think of all the ways you want to be successful.

What size boat would you need to hold the *quality* and *quantity* of success you desire? Could all your success fit on a dinghy, or would it sink under the weight? How about a sleek sailboat? Maybe a yacht would be big enough?

You might think that you'd be comfortable with just a dinghy's worth of success, but even a few minor successes could make that dinghy ride pretty low. If water is already sloshing over the gunwales, more success could sink the whole caboodle.

What you need is a bigger boat! The bigger the boat, the more success it can hold. And make sure there's plenty of room for future success—for success you haven't even dreamed of yet.

So there you are, standing at the end of the dock, scanning the horizon. The thought of all that success makes you tingle with anticipation. Suddenly, you see it! Your Success Ship!

A beautiful luxury liner is heading straight for you, cutting majestically through the water. As it draws closer, the sun illuminates the gold letters painted on the bow: *S U C C E S S*. And below it, your name in golden script, just the way you sign it. There's no doubt about it—this is *your* Success Ship.

Moving swiftly and gracefully through the water, your ship pulls closer and closer. The closer it gets, the more excited you become. You jump up and down on the dock, cheering and whistling.

Your Success Ship blows its whistle three times to announce its arrival, and pulls up smoothly alongside the dock. On deck you see every kind of success you want. Masses of success are piled high. People important to your success are on deck, and wave to you excitedly.

The people on board hoist you up on deck. They applaud you and gather around to shake your hand. You thank them for their help and encouragement, and together you celebrate the arrival of your success. Someone pops open a bottle of champagne and a band strikes up your favorite tune. You dance around the decks looking at all your success and bursting with joy!

Whenever success seems far away, picture your Success Ship sailing majestically toward you, getting closer and closer. Then feel the excitement of its arrival. Stand in the bow knowing that you are the captain of your Success Ship.

2

THINK BIG

This is your chance to think big—even huge. The way to do it is to start by thinking small—even tiny—and then let the thought grow.

You probably have a fairly decent list of things you want, ranging from the specific (that new car) to the abstract (creativity), and from the basic (shelter) to the miraculous (love).

From your long list of wants, choose one goal and form a mental picture of you having it. Say it's that new car you've been hankering after. Picture the exact make, model, year, and color of car you want. Picture yourself in the driver's seat, so that your subconscious is sure to get the message that this one's for you.

Once you've formed the picture, see it out in front of you at about a 45-degree angle below your line of sight—about waist high. Whatever the size of the picture was when it came to mind, reduce it to about the size of a postage stamp. Forms and colors are visible, but not details.

Then, as if you were enlarging a photograph, picture a larger picture. Jump it up to a 3 by 5 so that you can see more details.

Enlarge the picture again to a 4 by 6, a 5 by 7. Details are coming into crisp focus. If anything in the picture needs touching up or changing, now's the time to do it.

Once changes are made and imprinted, jump the picture up to an 8-by-10 glossy. The colors achieve a richness of hue. Details leap out. The grin that you picture on your face as you sit behind the wheel of your new car gets bigger. Detailing on the car is discernible.

Without losing resolution and definition, enlarge the picture to poster size. You're really seeing the big picture now. You might even want to add a caption on the poster, "Me and My New Car," or see your signature in a corner. The poster-sized picture reveals details about the clothes you have on, and that favorite ring you're wearing. You can actually read the gauges on the dashboard. The gas gauge reads Full and the odometer has a little over one hundred miles on it. The license plate has been issued by the state in which you live.

You like what you see. Suddenly you realize that you're seeing the car from all angles: from outside and inside, from front to back, from above and below. The image before you is no longer a flat two-dimensional photograph, but has rounded and filled so that it has depth. It has become three-dimensional and life-sized. It stands as tall as you and is luminous with light.

From being static, the picture of what you want shifts into motion. You watch your new car glide smoothly through the landscape. Look at the speedometer and see what it reads.

As you look at the dashboard of the car, you suddenly feel yourself looking at it from the driver's seat. You're really in the picture now. Feel the car accelerating forward. Feel the steering wheel gripped in your hands. What music do you have playing on the radio? Breathe in that new-car smell. Honk for happiness.

You simultaneously *feel* yourself driving your new car, and *see* yourself doing it. You're both the observer and the participant.

As the observer, fill the scene of what you want with crisp details and clear, bright light. As the participant, fill the scene with the clear, bright joy of having what you want. You're in the picture and the picture is yours.

Whenever you want something, start with a small picture of it, and then think big. You'll get the picture!

3

$$$ POOL

Here's a phrase you hardly ever hear: "No, no, I don't want any more money." No matter how much you have, there always seems to be a use for more. Or maybe you've got a case of the "Where Has All the Money Gone?" blues. The following imagery will help increase the amount of money flowing into your life.

You're standing at the edge of an empty swimming pool on a beautiful, sunny day. With your mind's eye notice details about the pool. What shape is it? What color? Is it edged with tiles or stone? What does the area around the pool look like? Are there lounge chairs? Maybe some big fluffy towels?

This is your pool, but it's going to be filled with money instead of water, so whatever you like about the pool—keep! Whatever you don't like—change.

Make the pool whatever shape suits your fancy. If the hue of blue isn't to your liking, change it. If you have a favorite good-luck symbol, incorporate it into the design of the pool. The tiles around the edge of the pool might spell out, "I easily receive abundant money." Have the towels monogrammed with your initials and dollar signs.

How big is your $$$ POOL? How deep? Is it big enough to swim laps in, or is it a shallow wading pool? Decide whether you want to be only knee-deep in money, or have enough to dive into. Make your $$$ POOL as big and deep as you want.

At one end of the pool are the pumps to fill the pool with money. Turn on the money pumps and let the $$$ flow in. Or have a sculpted cherub head that spouts a steady stream of $$$ from its mouth.

Money begins to fill the pool. Watch the $$$ level rise. What sound does it make as it flows in? Feel the excitement of having money pouring into your life.

When the pool is full of money, dive into it. Do a running

cannonball leap from the edge, or a graceful dive from a diving board. What does it feel like when you hit the $$$?

Your $$$ POOL is now big enough, deep enough, and full enough to support you. Splash happily in the crisp, clean new bills. What denomination are they? Picture $100 bills. Picture $1,000 bills.

Swim a few laps, feeling yourself moving through the money. What do the bills feel like against your skin? What sound do they make? What do they smell like? Lie on your back and float on the money. Play *in* it. Play *with* it.

Enjoy the money! Think of the fun you can have with it. Feel how delightfully satisfying it is to have enough money to take care of all your needs and wants. If there are family and friends you want to share your money with, invite them into the pool.

Visualize your $$$ POOL once a week. If the picture that first comes to mind shows a drop in the level of money, just turn on the pumps and let more money flow in. Then dive in and have fun.

4

MAKE IT REEL

You've heard the expression, "What you see is what you get." It's particularly true when it comes to visualizing what you want. Whatever you see in your mind is what you get. If the mental picture isn't clearly focused, or is poorly lit, or lacks important details, you'll end up with something sorta like what you had in mind, but frustratingly wrong. The more clearly and completely you visualize what you want, the sharper the picture is that you send to your subconscious, and the better your chances are of getting what you want.

Imagine yourself as the writer, producer, director, and star of the movie of your life. Is it an action-adventure film? A romantic comedy? A drama or a mystery? The story is being shot scene by scene, and there's an important scene coming up that you especially want to go smoothly. By making the scene clear and complete on the movie reel in your mind, you'll help make it real.

Think about the upcoming scene. Where does it take place? Who, besides you, will be in it? What will the main action be? What will the cast say to one another? How will they move and interact? How will you light the scene so that everyone and everything can be clearly seen?

Go over the scene to make sure that you haven't left out anything important. When you're satisfied with the staging, casting, action, and dialogue, you're ready to film.

Scout the location and clear it of anyone or anything that might interfere with filming. This could mean getting rid of disruptive or lazy people, negative attitudes, limiting beliefs, bad weather, etc. Ask your production crew to help you.

Assemble the cast, handing them their scripts, which you have written. Tell them the purpose of the scene, explaining your motivation for doing it. Answer any questions so that everyone is clear about the role he or she is to play. Be sure to include yourself in the scene.

When all the actors know their lines and the scene has been blocked out, they take their places. You, the director, shout, "Action!" The cameras roll and the scene unfolds smoothly. You, the cast, and crew work together in harmony.

When the scene is completed, yell, "Cut!" Cast and crew turn to you and applaud, and you in turn applaud them.

Go to the screening room to watch the dailies. Imagine sitting on a wide, plush seat in a dark, intimate theater with members of the cast and crew. On the armrest of your seat is a console of buttons. You push the one marked "Projection." The film rolls and the screen lights up. The title of the scene appears over a long shot of the location you just filmed. Then the camera zooms in for a close-up of the action. Every person and detail are in sharp focus. The light is bright, the colors vivid. All lines are clearly spoken, and the action unfolds exactly as you wrote it, directed it, and acted it.

Sitting there watching what you've created, you feel successful and satisfied. A rush of elation almost floats you right up out of the seat. You can feel the light of success shining brightly on you, just as the light of the scene you've created shines brightly on the screen.

At the end of the scene everyone turns to you and applauds for a job well done, and you in turn applaud them. As the writer, producer, director, and star of your life you have successfully made the reel scene real.

5

TAKING OUT THE GARBAGE

Computer programmers have a saying: "Garbage in, garbage out." That means that if you program garbage information into the computer system, garbage information is what you'll get out. The same is true for you. If you program garbage thoughts and garbage feelings into your subconscious, garbage is what you'll get in your life.

Unfortunately, just as day-to-day living produces physical garbage—empty boxes, blackened banana peels, crumpled paper—it also produces mental and emotional garbage. Empty hopes, blackened attitudes, and crumpled feelings accumulate, no matter how tidy and healthy you are. This subconscious garbage can stink up your life, and as it takes up more and more space it gets in the way of you getting your goals. Either the garbage spills across the door preventing it from opening when opportunity knocks, or it becomes piled so high that you can't even see your goal.

When was the last time you took out your mental and emotional garbage? Imagine that it's overflowing the cans and wastebaskets in the various rooms of your home: kitchen, bedroom, bathroom, den, workshop. What does your garbage look like? Rotten eggs of plans never hatched? Bones from dreams that died? Tangled strings of frustration? Broken glass and rusty nails of anger? Sad wads of used Kleenex? Or maybe the garbage has been lying around for so long that it's no longer even recognizable. Collect the garbage from every room in your mental house. Whatever the symbolic images, let them rise up from your subconscious into your conscious mind. As the garbage surfaces, throw it into heavy-duty, three-ply, industrial-strength plastic garbage bags. Use as many bags as it takes to do the job—you might need only one bag; you might need twenty. As you fill the bags with your mental and emotional garbage, tie them shut with a knot or a twist-tie.

As soon as the last garbage can or wastebasket has been emptied, and all the bags are full and tied, you hear a garbage truck rumble to a stop outside. You call to the garbage collector to help you carry the garbage bags out to the truck. The garbage collector could be anyone: a garbage man, a woman, a cartoon hero, a famous historical person, an athlete, or even an animal.

The two of you lug the garbage bags out to the waiting truck. You can hear the truck's compactor grinding away. As you heave the bags into the truck, each bag is squeezed, chewed, and swallowed up.

When the last bag of mental and emotional garbage has disappeared into the bowels of the truck, the garbage collector slaps the side of the truck to signal the driver to take off. You thank the garbage collector for his help and wave to him as the garbage truck lumbers away. Watch the truck until it rounds a corner and disappears from sight.

Walking back into the house, you notice that there's more bounce in your step. You mind feels free and light. Your heart breathes more easily. Entering your home, you walk through each room. Every garbage can and wastebasket is satisfyingly empty, refreshingly clean. No more stink. No more garbage to get in the way of what you want.

You decide that from now on, whenever mental and emotional garbage starts accumulating, you're going to throw it out before it causes clutter and starts stinking up your life. The garbage collection schedule is flexible to suit your needs, and there'll always be someone on the truck to help.

6

LIGHT–MIGHT

Light is essential, active, and powerful. It illuminates, helping us to see and be seen. It lights the way to knowledge. It encourages growth, both metaphorically and literally. Without sunlight there'd be little growth, and what there was would probably have the IQ of a mushroom.

Light casts out darkness because darkness cannot exist in the same space as light. Darkness isn't necessarily negative, but it can be. Darkness can represent a limiting belief or attitude, an emotion destructively expressed, exploitation, a lack of knowledge, inertia, or an absence of love.

The following visualization will help increase the quantity and quality of light in your life so you can be imbued with light-might.

About a yard in front of you, between your chest and your forehead, picture, or sense, a small ball of light about the size of a Ping-Pong ball. It's bright white and glimmers with energy. It vibrates with power. It hums with potency. Even though it's small, it shines with such intensity that it lights up a large area around it. It lights up you.

As this ball of vibrating white light floats in mid-air in front of you, bobbing slightly as if eager, you begin to feel an inner glow. It seems to tickle your sense of fun and makes you feel optimistic. You wish the ball were bigger. The instant you have that thought, the ball of light begins to expand. It grows to the size of a honeydew melon, then to the the size of a dinner plate. It expands to volleyball size. You realize that you can make the ball of light as big and bright as you want, just by thinking about it.

The ball of light grows bigger and brighter until it's just slightly taller and wider than you are. The light has powerful magnetic appeal and draws you to it. You step into the light as easily as stepping into your living room, and it feels just as familiar. As soon as you enter the light, you feel simultaneously excited and peaceful.

You're sparked by the idea that anything you want to have, or do, or be, is possible. Yet at the same time you feel relaxed, confident that what you want will come to you.

You both hear and feel the hum of the light. Pinpoint bursts of light dance around you, tickling your fancy. You feel bubbly, like a glass of champagne. The light shines on you and through you, realigning energy, revitalizing, healing. It sparks ideas. You feel whole and healthy. Protected. Empowered.

You realize that the high energy of the light creates such a strong magnetic field that as long as you're filled and surrounded with the light, it will attract what you want. Think of something concrete you want to have—money, love mate, job, computer, car, home, etc.—and picture it in front of you, just beyond the light. Let yourself really want it so that you beam brightly with desire, shining your light on the object of your desire and drawing it to you. The light expands to completely surround your goal. You have illuminated, attracted, and protected your goal.

Step into your ball of light the first thing every day. By putting yourself in the light you can see and be seen more clearly, feel energized, attract what you want, solve problems more easily (because you see the light), and avoid or reduce mishaps.

It's also helpful to put a ball of light around anyone or anything in your life that you want to protect or empower: loved ones, friends, employers, doctors, your car, airplanes, your home, your work site, meetings, letters, business projects, your checkbook, investments, etc. There's plenty of light to go around.

Light is powerful and empowering. When you surround and fill yourself with bright, white light-might, more things go right!

7

STATE OF SUCCESS

Success is a state of mind. So is failure. If you've been living in a state of failure, now's as good a time as any to move to the state of Success, just as you might move to the state of California.

What does your state of Failure look like? Is it a barren state where nothing grows? Dry brown dirt stretching in all directions? A dead tree trunk silhouetted against the gray, overcast sky: a dream that tried and failed? Rubble lying about in heaps, and rusted car carcasses littering dead-end roads? People trudging aimlessly, eyes glued to the ground, going nowhere?

As you shuffle through the state of Failure you see a sign announcing: "State of Success, 4 blocks." An arrow points to the right. You perk up at the thought that the state of Success could be so close.

The first block is a block-long stretch of a child's wooden alphabet blocks. The letters spell out a belief or attitude you have that blocks you from being successful. It might say, "Success corrupts." Or, "I don't deserve success." Turn over the blocks until they spell out the opposite belief. "Success enlivens." "I deserve success." You've made it past the first block.

The second block represents a feeling that has been blocking you, such as fear, anger, hate, etc. You might see a block-long block of ice, or a block of burning wood, or a block of steel. Imagine ways to melt the ice, put out the fire, or demolish the steel. Be creative and forceful about it.

The third block is made of brick. You can see the marks left on the wall from when you banged your head in the past. But now, instead of running into the brick wall, you walk alongside it. In no time at all you're at the end and past it.

The fourth block is a jumble of block-high, unlit neon tubing. You see a switch and turn it on. The neon lights up, announcing to everyone near and far, "I, (your name), Choose Success." The sign is so bright and colorful that it makes you feel bright and colorful, too.

After you've passed the last block you come to the border between Success and Failure. It isn't the mountainous thicket of thorns you thought it would be; it's just a simple white line painted across the road. A man with a clipboard comes over and asks, "What business do you have in the state of Success?" Firmly you tell him that you have plenty of business. He nods his head and asks if any family or friends will be coming over? You give him their names. He doffs his cap to you and wishes you the best as he waves you across the state-of-mind line.

You step over the line. It's easy. A large sign says,

Entering Success
Population: Unlimited

Everywhere around you the earth is covered with a blanket of lush, green grass. Flowers fill the air with the sweet smell of Success. Graceful trees, thick with leaves and fruit, arch into the clear blue sky: dreams that are alive and growing. Tall buildings and prosperous homes line the streets and avenues.

The inhabitants of Success walk with purpose, their gaze on the future. There is a lilt to their step and a gleam in their eyes. Glowing with health, they smile easily and often.

Inhale a deep lungful of the sweet air of Success. It energizes you and sparks initiative. You, too, walk with purpose, eyes looking ahead with a sparkle. Smiling easily, you know that you're going to be successful. You let out a whoop of triumph and joy, so glad to have moved to the state of Success!

8

SEA SEE

There's something you've been wanting. Maybe it's that job offer, or a lifetime love mate, or money, or a new home or car. You've been wanting it so hard that it almost hurts. You're tense with expectancy; you ache with anticipation.

Take a break from longing. Imagine that you go down to the sea—just to see what you can see. Hear the waves slapping against the shore as you approach. Take off your shoes and stand barefoot on the sand or a rocky outcropping, letting the waves wash over your feet. The water feels refreshing.

Soothed by the sound of the sea and the gentle waves lapping around your feet, you begin to relax. The tension within you ebbs out from your feet into the water, and is carried out to sea where it dissolves. Your muscles relax. The knot in your stomach loosens. The ache in your heart disappears. The tightness in your mind relaxes.

Closing your eyes, draw in a deep breath, filling your lungs with fresh, salty air. Exhale whatever tension is left. Take deep breaths, exhaling powerfully, until you feel every bit of tension leave. The fresh air enriches your blood and your brain with oxygen, and you feel especially alert.

With your physical and mental eyes still closed, picture what it is you want. But this time there's no tension associated with it. Instead, the image of what you want floats lightly to mind with a playful air. Be sure to picture yourself in the same picture with what you want, being delighted to have it. You might see yourself sharing it with someone special, or having friends congratulate you. As you're picturing what you want, it feels very real and right, and, best of all, relaxed.

You open your mental eyes, and, to your surprise, what you want is floating on the sea in front of you. There's your boss standing on the bow of a yacht holding out a contract to you. Or your love mate is rowing ashore with sure, steady strokes. Packets of $100 bills wrapped in cellophane cover the surface of the sea, bobbing merrily on the waves. Your new home or car is on a large barge that's being guided to shore by tugboats.

This is true bounty of the sea, and it's riding the waves right to you. You're ecstatic! You marvel at how easy it was to see your goals and manifest them. You're so excited that you jump up and down and do a happy little dance.

Shake your boss's hand and accept the contract, signing it with a flourish and a thank you. Or throw your arms around your love mate's neck and give him or her a big kiss. Your love mate takes your hand and you walk along the shore together. The packets of money float toward you and you load them in a string of dinghies with your name painted on the bows. The car lands on the beach, you start 'er up, and drive happily away. The key is in the door to your house, and, as you turn it, you and the house are transported to the foundation waiting at your ideal spot.

Whenever you want something, go down to the sea. Then relax and see what you want. The sea will carry it to you on swift, strong currents. It's easy to see at the sea.

9

WHAT GOES AROUND
COMES AROUND

You may have heard the saying, "What goes around, comes around," meaning that what you put into motion comes back to you. The saying is based on the concept that what you think, and do, and say, attracts more of the same. That being true, it is definitely worth your while to send out the most positive thoughts possible, so that positive energy returns to you.

The following visualization is used to send out strong positive thoughts about something you want more of in order to magnetize yourself to attract what you want. The goal could be love, money, joy, health, success, confidence, inspiration, etc.

Say you want more joy in your life. Choose a symbol or image for joy and visualize it. Make it clear and simple. It could be a symbol like a radiant star, or an arrow pointing up, or an ever-flowing waterfall. It might be a picture of you jumping for joy.

After you have your image of joy clearly in mind, feel the energy of joy. Let it sing and dance inside you. Think of the positive effects of having joy in your life. How the more joy you have, the more joy you'll attract, and the more joy you'll enjoy.

Let the energy of joy build and expand. Picture your symbol for joy in your mind and pour your emotional energy into the symbol until the image comes alive. See it glow. Feel it vibrate. Place your symbol for joy, glowing with energy, to your left and say, "Joy is to my left." Feel it there.

Then see and feel your symbol for joy to your right. Say, "Joy is to my right."

See and feel joy in back of you, protecting you. Say, "Joy is behind me."

See and feel joy in front of you, guiding you. Say, "Joy is before me."

See and feel joy underneath you, supporting you. Say, "Joy is below me."

See and feel joy over your head, sheltering you. Say, "Joy is above me."

When you have placed joy all around you, experience what it feels like to be completely surrounded by joy. Know that joy is available to you in all directions. Feel the abundance and the power of being encircled with joy. Say, "Joy is all around me."

Then draw the image and the energy of joy into yourself, absorbing it into your mind and into your heart. Say, "Joy is within me." Let it fill every nook and cranny of you so that your very fingers and toes feel joyful. Even your ears feel joyful.

The feeling of being filled and surrounded by what you want is sheer fun. This is an excellent visualization to do in the morning to get the day off to a good start. The more you put positive thoughts of what you want into motion, the more what you want will come to you. What goes around, comes around.

10
PLUGGED IN

Ever have one of those days when you feel totally disconnected? Out of touch with friends, family, work, life, yourself? Or maybe you're having one of those weeks when it seems as if some invisible saboteur has pulled the plug on every project you've been working on so diligently. If things are disconnected and no electricity is flowing to light up your life, here's a way to get plugged in again.

Picture your place of power, that place in your mindscape where you feel safe, strong, and sure. Somewhere in your place of power, picture a tower of power. It might look like a cross between an electric company's power station and the Eiffel Tower. The coils, generators, and transistors buzz and crackle with energy. As you stand in front of the tower of power, bending your head back to see the top of the spire rising into the clouds, it generates so much energy that you can feel it on your skin like static electricity. This is your private power source.

At the base of your tower of power is a room marked "Goals, Aspirations, and Relationships." Entering the room you see that the walls are covered with rows of electrical sockets. Above each socket is a plaque identifying the purpose of the socket. The plaques are inscribed with the names of family members, friends, work-related people and projects, health goals, desired personal qualities, etc. For example, a row of plaques might read "Mom, Dad, Fred, Susie Q., Tattinger Account, Mr. Gordon, $20,000, Flat Stomach, Vitality, Patience, Vacation."

These sockets are for anyone and anything that is important to you. (It doesn't have to be important to anyone else—just to you.) Check the plaques to make sure that they're up to date. Change them, erase them, or add new ones until you're satisfied.

Some of the sockets have plugs in them, some are empty, and some plugs are just lying on the floor. Seeing which sockets have plugs in them and which don't will tell you where you've been putting energy, and where you need to put energy. Each plug is attached to your tower of power, with a plug for every socket, so grab a plug and plug it where you want it, until all the sockets have plugs in them.

Check the indicator lights on the sockets. The indicator light comes on as soon as you push a plug in, and stays on to let you know that energy is flowing. If the light doesn't come on, take out the plug and reinsert it, or flip the on/off switch to on. What color are the indicator lights? Are there different colors for different people and goals?

Step back and look at all the glowing lights. You're plugged in and ready to go. Check the sockets periodically to make sure that everyone and everything important to you is plugged in and receiving energy from your tower of power. If plugs have been disconnected, plug them back in. If you want to disconnect from someone or something, pull the plug and erase the name from the plaque. When new people and projects come into your life, make new plaques and plug in. Keep what's important to you humming with energy by staying plugged in.

II

SEAL OF APPROVAL

One of the underpinnings of the American philosophy is the belief, based on the Protestant work ethic, that hard work shall not go unrewarded. No matter what your religion, you've probably been making an effort to succeed. You've done everything you know—defined what you want, taken appropriate steps, thought positively—but success continues to be just beyond your reach. It's a frustrating situation, to say the least.

Sometimes, the last remaining step, the one that sends success sliding into your grasp, is permission to succeed. Picture someone in your life—past or present, dead or alive—from whom you need (for whatever reason) permission to succeed. It could be your father, grandfather, mother, sibling, friend, lover, sixth-grade teacher, or someone who is directly involved in your success.

Picture, or sense, the person standing in front of you. See him as clearly as possible, noticing some distinctive feature: the color of his eyes, a crooked front tooth, a favored piece of jewelry, big feet, the way he holds himself.

Say hello and call him by name. Ask him for permission to succeed. His reaction to your request will reveal something about the nature of your relationship with him. He might do anything from telling you to get lost to affably agreeing.

If his response is negative, don't accept it! Say, "I insist that you give me permission to succeed!" Say, "I *demand* that you give me permission to succeed! I deserve it!" Say, I *command* you to give me permission to succeed!"

You insistently persist until he agrees to give you permission. Hear him say loud and clear, "I (his name) give you (your name) permission to succeed." Make him put it in writing. You just happen to have a Permission to Succeed certificate with you. In the lower right-hand corner is a large golden-sunburst seal of approval. His name and yours are already typed in. You sign it and date it, then give it to him to sign. After he's signed, he officially stamps the certificate "APPROVED" in bold, block letters. Or the stamp might say, "A-OK," or "MIGHTY FINE," or "GO FOR IT," or "IT'S YOURS." He hands you the Permission to Succeed certificate to keep and you thank him for approving it.

Demand permission to succeed from every person who you feel has the power to grant it. If he agrees right away, great! If the person resists, insist until you hold the signed, dated, sealed, and stamped certificate in your hand.

And last but not least, obtain permission to succeed from yourself. See yourself standing proudly in front of you. Notice some special feature about yourself. Say hello. Ask yourself for permission to succeed. You give it—signed twice by you, sealed, stamped, and delivered. "I (your name) give (your name) permission to succeed." Put *your* Permission to Succeed certificate with the others.

Whenever success seems just beyond your reach, see if there's anyone who's withholding permission. Add that certificate to the stack you already have, and read each one.

Spread the certificates with their seals of approval around you in a circle so that you're completely surrounded by permission. Or have each person from whom you have obtained permission stand behind his certificate and repeat the proclamation giving you permission to succeed.

Knowing in your mind and in your heart that you have permission to succeed, you'll be able to reach out and grab success— efficiently, effortlessly, effervescently. Enjoy!

12

WOULD CARVING

Is there something you've been wanting for a while, but it just never seems to happen? You have a sneaking suspicion that whatever's preventing you from getting what you want might have something to do with you, but you can't quite put your finger on it; you would if you could. This visualization will help put you in touch with whatever attitude or behavior pattern is keeping you from getting what you want.

In your mind's eye, see, or sense, yourself walking along a white sand beach at twilight. The beach is deserted except for sandpipers leaving their tracks in the wet sand. The only sound you hear is waves breaking and rushing over the sand.

A recent storm has cleansed the air, making it especially invigorating. Flotsam and jetsam, churned up by the stormy sea, are strewn along the shore. Strolling along the water's edge you find shells and bits of colored glass frosted by the saltwater. A spiraled nautilus shell gleams from under some seaweed.

Just ahead, a large plank of wood, its edges rounded by the sea, attracts your attention. As you bend down to look at it you notice that the first letter of your first name is carved in the wood. Wonderingly, you trace the ornately carved letter with your finger.

Half of the thick plank is buried deep in the sand. You grab hold of the end that's sticking out and pull. It's heavy and you need to use both hands. The wood feels velvety soft, having been sanded smooth by the sea.

With some effort you pull the plank free. The end that was buried in the sand is wet, and darker than the part of the plank that was exposed to the sun—the part that had your initial on it. There, on the section that was buried, is another carving.

As you brush away the sand that clings wetly to the board, the details of the carving become clear. The carving describes—in word, or symbol—what it is that you're doing, or thinking, or feeling, that prevents you from getting what you want. Maybe the word *stubborn* is carved in the wood, or a carving of a mule. Or the word *closed*, or a carving of a closed door.

Whether it's a word or a picture, as soon as you see it you know the truth of it. But instead of feeling sad about it, you feel glad, because now that you can identify the problem you can do something about it. The more you let the truth sink in, the happier and freer you feel. Just as you freed the heavy plank from the sand, your honesty frees you from whatever was burying your success.

Still curious, you turn the plank over, and there, carved on the damp underside, is another word or picture. This one depicts a quality or action that is opposite to the one on the first side. Instead of *stubborn*, the word is *flexible*, or a carving of a gymnast. Or the word, *open*, or a carving of an open door.

Take the plank home with you and put it up on your bedroom wall to remind you of your new, positive attitude. You'll know when you've made the change from the old to the new because you'll achieve what you wanted. Celebrate by burning the plank.

13

THE WORD FOR TODAY

Has your mouth been full of words like *failure, lonely, broken, sick, unloved,* or *poor*? Have you had to eat those words and don't like how they taste, not to mention the fact that they have no nutritional value?

Change your word diet to one that's delicious and nutritious. First spit out the words that taste bitter and rubbery. Spit out *failure*. Spit out *sick*. Do it forcefully, saying things like, "Yuck!" "That tastes awful!" "Pattooey!" Rinse the aftertaste out of your mouth.

What's the good word? Think of a word that best describes how you'd like to be. *Successful. Loved. Loving. Wealthy. Healthy. Wise. Confident. Free. Creative. Productive.*

Let's say that you want more love in your life. Picture, or sense, the word *love* on a plate in front of you as if it were food. Is it covered with frost from being frozen? Thaw it out and cook it until it's steaming hot.

With your mind's eye look at the word *love*. How big are the letters? Are they in a small mound off to the side, like peas, or do they cover the plate? If your *love* letters look puny and putrid, change them so they look temptingly appetizing. Give yourself a generous portion.

What color are the letters? Dark or light? Bland or muddy? Make them a tasty color. They can be the color of corn, carrots, strawberries, candy canes, taffy, or sweet potatoes.

What does *love* smell like? Is it fragrant like a freshly baked cake? Aromatic like a hearty stew simmering on the stove? Sweet? Earthy? Tart? Pungent?

What kind of sound does the word *love* make? Does it sizzle? Does it bubble? Does it hum? Does it whistle? Does it fizz?

Reach out and touch the *love* letters. What do they feel like? Yielding or firm? Fuzzy or smooth? Wrinkled? Velvety? Warm or cool?

Break off a piece of *love*. What consistency is it? If it's stringy and tough, sprinkle some tenderizer on it. Does it crumble like cake, or is it spongy? It could stretch like taffy or be crisp like a radish.

Put the piece in your mouth. What flavor is *love*? Is it sweet? Refreshingly minty? Chew it or simply let it dissolve.

The *love* you want can be eaten however you want. You might be so hungry for *love* that you gulp it down in one bite—just don't eat so fast that you wind up with indigestion. Try breaking off pieces and nibbling them bit by bit, or eat the word a letter at a time.

Use all your senses to savor your word for the day. See it. Smell it. Hear it. Touch it. Taste it.

Whenever the words in your mouth taste sour, spit them out and serve yourself up a new, tasty word. Make a complete meal out of it. Pick a word for the day and eat it. Digest it. Be nourished by it. You can eat the same word for days in a row, or vary your diet to suit your taste. A good word a day keeps the blues away.

14
YES

If you're a living, breathing, thinking human being, chances are there's something you want. It might be something you want to have. Or do. Or be.

Chances are also good that while part of you is saying, "Yes, go for it!" another part is saying, "No!" That ornery inner voice tries to convince you that you really don't deserve what you want. Or, it whines, "If you get it, you'll be sorry. It'll be so much work, so much responsibility."

If your *no* voice is louder and more insistent than your *yes* voice, chances are you'll miss out on getting what you want. What you need is a unanimous *yes* from your inner voice. A *yes* to success!

With your mind's eye, picture, or sense, the entrance to where you live. On the front door, in huge, dark letters, is the word *no*. Rip those letters off the door and break them into pieces. Throw them in the trash.

Picture letters for the word *yes*. Make them whatever size and color you want—the bigger and brighter the better. Put the Y E S letters up on the door so that they greet you when you come home, then step back and admire your handiwork.

Open the door and go into your living room. The first thing you see is Mr. No lounging on your sofa. He looks slovenly and angry. He's munching crackers in the shape of little *N*'s and *O*'s, and scattering crumbs all over your floor.

Say "*No!*" to Mr. No. Kick him off the sofa and boot him out the door. Invite in a healthy, happy, agreeable *yes*. Be sure to vacuum up all the crumbs.

Dominating your living room wall is a large, ugly picture of the word *no*. Take it down and tear it up. Throw it in the trash. In its place, hang a pleasing, colorful picture of the word *yes*. Notice how it brightens up your living room.

Go through every room in your house. Wherever you see a *no*, throw it out and replace it with a *yes*.

When you brush your teeth, if you see a *no* reflected in the bathroom mirror, wipe it off. Picture a *yes* shining back at you.

Does a scatter rug have an unattractive *no* design? Give the *no* the old heave-ho. Replace it with an attractive non-slip *yes* rug.

If a pot of *no* is brewing on the stove in the kitchen, dump it out. Make a fresh pot of *yes*.

At night, are you sleeping with a *no* stretched out beside you? Kick it out. Sleeping with a *yes* curled up next to you is much more satisfying.

Get in the habit of picturing a *yes* wherever you are.

When you're driving, sit a *yes* next to you. Picture a gleaming, silver *yes* as a hood ornament.

Have a *yes* sit across from your desk at work.

Eat all your meals with a *yes*. Eat *yes* cereal, and *yes*wiches, and *yes* soufflés.

Think *yes*! See *yes*! Feel *yes*! When your *yes* voice is loud and clear, getting what you want will be much, much easier!

15

PROSPERITY

It seems beyond the limits of possibility to imagine a world where everyone has the basics: food, shelter, clothing, health, work they enjoy, self-respect, love.

What? A world without poverty? Without crime? Without war? Fat chance. Where would be the challenge? The challenge would be in using the energy previously spent on war battles, and battling poverty and crime, to solve problems of a higher order, such as how to improve the quality of life for everyone.

There is a Native American tribe in Canada whose people believe that nothing happens on earth that isn't first imagined in the mind. If we can't imagine that worldwide prosperity is possible, chances are slim that anything even close to that will happen. Let's open our minds to the possibility of a planet where everyone is prosperous—not just financially, but physically, mentally, emotionally, and spiritually.

Imagine Mr. and Mrs. Santa Claus in a cargo plane stuffed with an unending supply of brightly gift-wrapped bundles. Each package has a name tag attached to the ribbon. Flying through the night ahead of the sun, Mr. and Mrs. Claus distribute gifts to everyone in the world. As they fly over cities, villages, and huts, they push the button that opens the door to the cargo hold, automatically releasing the gifts for the people in that area.

Each gift floats down to the right person. People don't even have to have been good to receive a gift; they're entitled to it just for being alive. When each person awakens—whether on bare ground or satin sheets—the gift is right by his or her head; it's the first thing the person sees.

Picture yourself awaking to see a brightly wrapped gift by your head. You check the tag: "For (your name), with Love." Yup, it's yours all right. You untie the ribbon and tear off the paper. Inside is a bundle of money—however much you need to get your life in order. A note is stuck under the band: "Please use this for your good."

The second part of the present is a golden good-luck charm that symbolizes the particular skill that was given to you at birth. Your talent could be in science, math, athletics, the arts, business, comedy, politics, etc. Wear the golden symbol (medal, dollar sign, caduceus, heart, waterfall, etc.) of your talent on a chain around your neck, or tucked in your pocket where you can rub it. The charm is to remind you of your talent, and to help you develop it.

The talent part of the gift is the one that will endure and sustain you. There's an old saying: "If you give a man a fish he eats for a day. If you teach a man how to fish, he eats for a lifetime." Money is the gift of fish. Talent is the gift of learning how to fish.

After opening your gift, imagine every person in the world— man, woman, young, old, rich, poor, healthy, sick, housed, unhoused, fat, thin, black, white, red, yellow, brown—receiving and opening his or her present. They can all use the money to improve their lives in the immediate future, and their talent to fulfill their lives into the distant future.

The thought that everyone on earth could have what he or she wants is an idea so bright it lights up your mind and makes your heart shine. A sense of calm delight spreads through you. The possibility of a prosperous planet becomes more probable once you think it. The more often you entertain the thought, the more welcome it becomes. Visualizing a prosperous planet is a gift to others, and to yourself!

IMAGE SHINING

16

BANKING ON YOU

Do you feel as if you've never done enough? Or haven't done it well enough? Are you forever nattering at yourself to do better? To be better?

Your subconscious keeps a tally of your self-esteem based on what you think of yourself. Every time you scold yourself, you make a withdrawal on your self-esteem account. And every time you give yourself credit for what you've done, you make a deposit.

It doesn't take a genius to figure out that if you make more withdrawals than deposits, you're going to end up physically, mentally, and emotionally bankrupt. If you feel sluggish and cranky, you could already be on your way to bankruptcy.

Use the following image to balance your self-esteem account. You might even consider building a nice little nest egg—putting something aside for those rainy days.

With your mind's eye, picture, or sense, yourself in a town. It looks friendly and prosperous. As you stroll along the sidewalk, people smile at you. You enjoy the architecture of the buildings.

Just ahead you see your bank. But it isn't just any bank, it is literally *your* bank. It says so on the front, in elegant gold letters: "The (your name) Bank and Trust Company."

Opening the front door, you go inside. The interior is spacious and full of light. Friends and business acquaintances are in line waiting to make transactions with you. You notice which ones are there to make deposits, which withdrawals.

The door to your office has your name on it, and below it, "PRESIDENT." Sitting down at your desk you check the balance sheet of your self-esteem account. The statement is in a ledger. Or filed in a cabinet. Or you call up the information on your computer.

What debits are itemized? Have you been thinking that you're worthless, mere bellybutton lint, because you didn't do a good enough job on a project? Or blew up at a friend? Or were late for an appointment? Or didn't exercise hard enough? Or because your nose is crooked? Or because you forgot to line up your shoes in your closet?

And what's entered in the credit column? A big fat zero? A goose egg instead of a nest egg? You'd better make a deposit—and fast—or you're going to be bankrupt.

Come on. You can't be *all* bad. At least you get up most mornings. Hey—some days that's definitely worth a pat on the back. And aren't you pretty good about brushing your teeth? What about that dog you petted? And the extra cookie you didn't eat? And the call you made to a sick friend? And the bright idea you put into action? And how about that goal you accomplished?

These all belong in the plus column, but unless *you* give yourself credit for them, consciously entering them, they won't register in your subconscious. So write your accomplishments in your self-esteem ledger, seeing them written in your handwriting, or enter them in a self-esteem data file in your computer.

Check your self-esteem account statement regularly. It can be daily or weekly, but check it! If more debits show up than credits, start balancing! Review the good things you've done—everything from the magnificent to the mundane—and make those deposits. Don't delay.

17

ROOM FOR HAPPINESS

Do you see yourself as a happy or unhappy person? If your image of yourself is unhappy, or if you're happy but would like to be happier, here's a visualization to help you make room for happiness.

Imagine that you're walking down a long corridor that has doors on either side; some are open, some are closed. Each door has a sign: "Success," "Love," "Wisdom," "Recognition," "Health," etc.

You're looking for the door marked "Happiness." When you reach it, the door is closed. Stand in front of it for a moment and take a couple of slow, deep breaths to relax. Turn the knob. Does it turn or is it locked? If it's locked, reach into your breast pocket, pull out the key to happiness, and open the door.

Is the room bright or dark? If it's dark, reach for the light switch next to the door and flip it on.

How large or small is the room? Is it the size of a broom closet full of dirty rags and dusty dreams? Expand the size of the room to make room for happiness—and lots of it. C'mon, try it; you might like it. Indulge yourself. You have nothing to lose but unhappiness.

How is the room furnished? Is it cozy or spartan? Make it comfortable. Picture a thick rug on the floor, in your favorite bright color. A sofa you can stretch out on for catnaps. An easy chair. Green, growing plants. A fireplace for those chilly days and nights. Fill the the room with whatever makes you happy.

What color are the walls? Gray? Black? Mud? See them painted a clear, soothing color. What's hanging on the walls? Black and white photos of you looking glum? Suffering? Failing? Struggling? Take every unhappy picture off the walls, break it over your knee, and throw it in the garbage can.

Now sit in your easy chair and create happy pictures of yourself in full color. The pictures range from wallet-sized to life-sized. Pictures of you laughing with family and friends, and being loved. Pictures of you being appreciated at home and at work. Smiling pictures of you enjoying the goals you've achieved. Healthy pictures of you looking the way you want to look. Pictures of you jumping for joy. Sitting in your easy chair, it's easy to create pictures of happiness.

Is there a window? Put one in. Put in several. Are the drapes closed and the shades pulled down? Open the curtains and pull up the shades. Let in the light. Open the windows and let in fresh air. Think big; put in French doors opening onto a terrace or balcony.

What's the view from the window? Dry desert or blooming meadow? Rocks or grass? Is it spring or winter? Give yourself a beautiful view, one that makes you happy to look at. Maybe a singing stream meanders under graceful shade trees. Beyond a lush forest, majestic mountains rise in the distance.

You have made room for happiness—allow yourself to be happy about it! Whenever you feel glum, picture the door to happiness being open, with sunlight spilling out into the corridor. Go in and create happiness—there's plenty of room for it now!

18

GETTING TO KNOW ME

Most of the time we're so busy *being* ourselves that we don't take time to *see* ourselves: we know how we are from the inside, but not from the outside. This visualization will help you see yourself from a more objective perspective. It's a bit challenging, because you alternate between being subjective and objective about yourself, but take it a step at a time and have fun with it.

Imagine that you call yourself on the phone. Do you call yourself so rarely that at first you can't remember your number? Dial your number and hear it ring. Whoops—did you get a recording because you're not home for yourself? What message do you want to leave?

Dial again. Darn, it's busy. Are you so busy talking to others that you don't have time to talk with yourself? Try one more time. It rings and this time you hear yourself answer, "Hello," the way you usually do. Ask, "How are you?" Listen to your answer.

Now invite yourself over. What? You don't want to see yourself? Why not? Is there something you don't like about yourself? Are you angry with yourself about something?

Find out what's preventing you from wanting to see yourself. Ask, "Why don't I want to see this person?" An answer will pop into your mind. Just asking the question tends to lower your resistance to seeing yourself. Hear yourself agree to come over.

Imagine yourself at home, waiting for you to arrive. You hear a knock at the door and open it. You're standing on the welcome mat. How do you look? Are you smiling? Are you glad to see yourself? What do you see about yourself that you like? What do you see that you don't like?

Invite yourself in and give yourself a big welcoming hug. How does it feel to hug yourself? Are you stiff and perfunctory about hugging, or receptive and friendly? Is it a close hug, or a distant one? Do you hug back?

Make yourself comfortable and ask if there's anything you can get you. A cup of kindness tea? A glass of fresh attitude? How about a plate of chocolate chip love cookies, or a loaf of home-baked bread buttered with laughter?

Use your imagination. What you ask for might be the real thing, or it might be symbolic of the emotional food you need. Whatever you want, you have it, and gladly bring it to yourself.

Sit down with yourself and chat. Get caught up on what's been going on. Ask how you're feeling. Talk about your dreams. Is there anything in particular that you want to say to yourself? Look yourself in the eye. What do you see? Are you comfortable with yourself? As you talk, reach out and gently touch yourself on the arm from time to time, as you would a friend.

After you've had a good talk with yourself, see yourself to the door. Hug yourself again—this time it's definitely close and warm. Thank yourself for such a heartwarming visit and invite yourself to come again soon.

This could be a somewhat difficult visualization to do the first couple of times you try it, because seeing yourself objectively is one of the more challenging aspects of getting to know who you are. But by getting outside yourself to see how you look and feel and think, you can make valuable discoveries about yourself. The better you know yourself, the better friend you can be to yourself—and others.

19

NEW CLOTHES

Have you ever had one of those days when you get up, get dressed, take a look at yourself in the mirror, and think, "Yech"? The image that's reflected back just doesn't make it; it doesn't match up with the way you'd like to look. Here's a way to change your inner image, which will then help to change your outer image.

Imagine standing in your bedroom in front of a full-length free-standing mirror: one of those honest ones that doesn't take off pounds. Check your reflection from head to toe. Nothing about you is to your satisfaction today. Your hair is messy and lacks sheen. Your face is drawn and gray. Your body is the wrong size and shape. Your clothes are ill-fitting and your shoes are dull. You lift up your foot and look at the bottom of it; yup—a hole in the sole.

Not a pretty picture, or a handsome one. You decide that this just won't do. Behind the mirror you notice a small door. You open it and have to stoop to squeeze through. Straightening up on the other side, you find yourself in a grassy meadow flooded with sunshine. In the center of the meadow is a deep natural pool of clear blue water that sparkles in the sunlight.

The pool looks inviting. You walk toward it, peeling off your old clothes. You kick off your worn-out shoes, sending them flying into the bushes.

Jump into the pool, or wade in gradually using the natural rock steps. Once in, the water is just the right temperature and feels so refreshing that it seems almost effervescent. As you soak in the clear blue of the pool, you are gently bathed clean. Physical aches and pains are soaked out. Even emotional pains disintegrate and float away. You bend your head back in the sparkling water and let it wash the dullness from your hair. Worries melt away.

Dirt, pain, and worry are replaced with exciting feelings of newness. You feel squeaky clean inside and out. You tingle with freshness. Energized, you step up and out of the pool.

Draped over the rocks that border the pool is a big fluffy towel and new clothes. You hurriedly dry yourself with the towel, giving your hair a fluff. Each article of clothing has a tag on it with your name. Your new clothes slip on smoothly, fitting the contours of your body as if they were tailor-made for you. You slip on burnished shoes so soft that they conform immediately to the shape of your feet.

Stepping up on a rock overlooking the pool, you look at your reflection in the water. From head to toe you like what you see. Your hair looks thick and healthy, and gleams in the sun. Your face has relaxed and your skin glows with health. Your body looks not too fat, and not too thin, but just right. The fabric, the style, and the color of your new clothes are exactly right for you. Your comfortable new shoes shine with a deep luster. You lift one foot and look at the bottom. The sole is whole.

This is your new image. Wear it well!

20

CHEERS

Are you feeling low because there's a gap between the way you are and the way you want to be? Is there some aspect of yourself that you'd like to change, but you just can't seem to work up the energy to get yourself off your duff and up to snuff? Use the following imagery to initiate change.

Imagine that you're sitting slouched over at the bottom of a rocky hill. The sky is overcast and everything looks gray. Gathered around the bottom of the hill are relatives, friends, and acquaintances. Mingling with the crowd are animals: dogs, lions, rabbits, bears, tigers, chimps, deer, and horses.

You feel as gray as the sky. You wish you were someone else, somewhere else. You think about what it is that you don't like about yourself. Maybe you think, "I'm lazy." Or "I'm a pessimist." Or "I'm overly critical." Or "I'm a loser." You think it to yourself in a sad, meek little thought-voice.

More than ever you wish you were someone else, somewhere else. Looking up you notice someone standing on top of the hill. The hill where the other person is standing is blanketed with bright flowers and sunshine instead of gray rocks and clouds. He or she stands proudly, feet planted firmly, back straight, head held high. There's something familiar about this person on top of the hill. You look more closely and realize that it's *you*. It's the person you want to be.

The person you want to be begins to speak in a confidant, powerful voice. "I'm glad to be here." Hear the crowd whistle its approval. Then he or she says, "I am ..." and completes the sentence with an adjective that's the *opposite* of the one you used before. "I'm *energetic*." Or, "I'm an *optimist*." Or, "I'm *tolerant*." Or, "I'm a *winner*." The crowd goes wild. Everyone applauds and cheers. The animals bark, and roar, and jabber.

From out of the crowd at the base of the hill, a horse trots up to you and whinnies encouragement. You jump up on the horse's back, grab his mane, and gallop up the hill. Feel the wind in your face. Feel the powerful movement of the horse underneath you. Hear the pounding of the horse's hooves against the earth. The rocks give way to gentle, grassy slopes. The gray sky turns to blue.

In no time at all you reach the top. The person you want to be smiles at you and welcomes you with open arms. As you embrace, you *become* the person you want to be. When you turn to face the crowd, you *are* the person you want to be. You feel confidant. Positive. You beam with joy because you like yourself. The crowd roars its approval. Looking down at their upturned faces you spot your mother and father, your grandparents, your best friend, your boss, your neighbors. They're all applauding you. A sense of accomplishment and well-being fills you.

Whenever you feel stuck being someone you don't want to be, get on your horse and ride to the part of yourself you *do* want to be. Hear the cheers resounding across the hills and valleys. Feel the glow of well-being within you, shining out.

21

POWER BACK

Somewhere along the line your self-confidence and self-esteem seem to have dropped to record lows. You're on the verge of total wimpdom, with no more motivation to succeed than a tranquilized hamster.

The cause of this malaise might be that you have unknowingly given your personal power away to someone. This is your *creative* power, not manipulative power. This is your power to act constructively, not to control others. But when you give your power away, you give others the ability to control you.

The remedy is to get your power back. Imagine yourself someplace where you feel safe, strong, and happy. It could be a room, a meadow, a bubble of light, a beach, etc. When you've settled into your place of power, ask yourself whom you might have given your power away to. The mental image of that person will pop into your mind. If there are several people who come to mind, pick the one you react to most strongly, or who seems the biggest. (You can use this visualization to get your power back from the others another time.)

Picture that person standing in front of you. It might be a parent, a lover, an ex-lover, a boss, a friend, a teacher—anyone with whom you've had a meaningful relationship. Tell the person that you mistakenly gave him your power, and you want it back. Be sure to tell him that he can keep his own power, but you want yours. How he reacts to your request will reveal the nature of your relationship with him. He may gladly give back your power. He may have hidden it somewhere. Or he may resist. If he resists, demand it back. Insist until he hands it over.

The form the power takes will be symbolic, and could also be indicative of some aspect of your relationship with that person. Maybe he hands you a glowing ball of light. Or a gift-wrapped package. Gold coins. A glass of crystal-clear water. A trophy, a crown, or jewelry. Or he could sprinkle you with diamond dust, or serve you your favorite food.

Reach out and take your power into your own hands. Then, with a sharp inhalation, suck it into you. Put it where it's most needed. You might breathe your power into your heart to heal and strengthen it, or into your mind for clarity, or into your throat for expression, or into some part of your body that wants to be healthier. If you don't have a sense of where to put your power, ask it where it wants to go.

When you have your power back, thank the person for returning it to you. Forgive him for holding onto it. And it's most important to forgive yourself for giving your power away in the first place. Understand that you probably did it because you wanted to be liked or loved, and you thought that was the way to do it. Be kind to yourself about having done it.

Be glad that you have your power back. Take a moment to feel how much better you feel. You abound with energy and confidence. You feel strong and centered. Capable. Optimistic. Glad to be alive. Ready for action. You *are* powerful!

22

BREAKING THE HABIT

Either life has crashed down on you forcing change, or through the growth process you have come to realize that a certain habit of yours has got to go. The habit—drugs, alcohol, cigarettes, sugar, etc.—is costing you more money, time, health, happiness, success, or all the above, than you can afford.

Whatever external guidance and support you choose to help you break your habit, the main change takes place internally. You're the one who chose to have the habit (allowing is choosing) and this empowers you to be the one who chooses to break it. Both choices begin within. This visualization offers some *internal* guidance and support to help you break the habit.

In your mind's eye, how do you see yourself in relation to your habit? Is your inner image that of you indulging in your habit? If it is, you're reinforcing the habit, not the change, and you're diminishing the positive effects of whatever external steps you're taking.

Make a mental picture of yourself engaged in your habit. It might be a slapdash sketch, or a muddy painting, or a black and white photograph. See it clearly, with as much detail as possible. Remember how unpleasant the aftereffects felt.

Break the engagement to your habit. Do this by picturing a black cord encircling you and your habit, binding the two of you together. Feel the tightness, the lack of freedom. Cut the cord. Sense the cord falling away. Feel the tension fall away, too. You breathe easier.

Now break the habit. Literally. The picture you made of you doing your habit is framed under glass in a scruffy black wood frame. Grab the picture with both hands and break it over your knee (but don't hurt yourself). Hear the glass break and the wood frame splinter. Tear the photo into tiny pieces, feeling the paper tear between your fingers. Hear it rip. Throw the whole mess—glass, frame, pieces of picture—into the garbage, or into an incinerator to burn.

The final step is to replace the habit-forming picture with two habit-*breaking* pictures. First see a vivid color photo of yourself refusing someone who's offering your habit. Hear yourself saying, "No, thanks." Don't say something like, "No, thanks, I'm trying to quit drinking [or snorting, or smoking, or over-eating], because that only reinforces the habit and the struggle to quit. Hear yourself say, "No, thanks, I don't do that." That's all. No righteousness needed, just a simple declarative statement.

The second color picture is of you engaged in doing something positive that's only possible if you've broken your habit. It might be a mental photograph of you receiving a paycheck, at home with a loving partner, exercising effortlessly, or fitting into a smaller-sized pair of pants.

Picture details. Make the colors bright. Surround your new inner images in new and beautiful gold frames. The more you look at the pictures, the bigger and brighter they become, until they're bigger and brighter than the old picture ever was. As the images expand, so does your joy. If you get the urge to jump for joy, give it a go.

Take the big, bright color picture of you enjoying the benefits of breaking your habit into the living room of your mind and hang it where you can look at it every day. Don't be surprised when the picture gets so big and vibrant that it expands into the third dimension.

The more you remind yourself of how you want to be, the more you'll become that person. When you can see yourself breaking the image of the old habit in your inner mental world, and see the benefits that result, it will be easier to see the same positive results in your external physical world.

23

LOTSA LUCK

"Boy, some people have all the luck!" Ever catch yourself saying or thinking that? How about making yourself the one with the luck? Here's how.

With your mind's eye, see, or sense, yourself in the middle of a lush green field. The sky overhead is a dome of blue. You hear birds singing, and a breeze blows gently around your face. The sweet, fertile smell of the earth delights you.

You're barefoot and the coolness of the earth soothes your soles. Glancing down, you notice the heart-shaped leaves of four-leaf clovers curling around the edges of each foot. You suddenly realize that the entire field is full of rich, green, lucky four-leaf clovers in all sizes. Some are as small as pennies and some are as big as dinner plates. Hundreds of thousands of lucky four-leaf clovers stretch as far as your eye can see.

The good-luck energy of the four-leaf clovers pushes up through the soles of your feet. It feels light and bubbly. It rises up your body to your knees, then to your hips and on up to your chest. Feel the lucky energy push up to your shoulders and flow down your arms to your hands. Your fingertips tingle with luck. The good luck bubbles up into your head like a fountain, refreshing your thoughts. You're filled with good luck from head to toe.

Lie down in the field of four-leaf clovers. They tickle your arms and legs and your feet, making you laugh with delight.

What do they smell like? Fill your lungs with the sweet smell of good luck, and let good luck spread throughout you body.

Pick a four-leaf clover and eat it. What does it taste like? Sweet and fresh? Minty? Earthy? You've just had a taste of good luck.

Play in the field. Roll over and over in good-luck clover. Good luck clings to your clothes and your skin. You're so happy that you feel like doing cartwheels and somersaults. Have a run of good luck.

Pick bunches of lucky four-leaf clovers. Make a bouquet of four-leaf clovers. Stuff your pockets with them.

Invite people you like to come and play in the field of lucky four-leaf clovers. Let *them* stuff their pockets with luck.

More four-leaf clovers will grow to replace the ones picked. In fact, you're in luck: the four-leaf clovers grow faster than you and all your friends can pick them.

Take all the lucky four-leaf clovers with you that you want. When you get home, put one wherever you want, to be reminded that good luck is yours easily and often. Keep some in your pocket. Put one on your front door, on your living room wall, on the bathroom mirror. Spread them around your bed at night. Sprinkle them on your checkbook, your family, your friends, your work desk. Put lucky four-leaf clovers wherever you want good luck to abound.

The field of lucky four-leaf clovers is yours for the seeing. Whenever your luck seems to have run out, visualize the field of four-leaf clovers, and go pick up some luck.

24

SHAPING UP

Are you in bad shape? Stiff with tension? Sagging with fatigue? Stooped with worry? Snippy with toxins? The following visualization will help shape you up inside and out.

With your mind's eye imagine that you're on a beach in a secluded cove. The water is clear and calm. Creamy cliffs rise up from the white sand. As you saunter along the beach the fine white sand makes a scrinching noise beneath your feet.

Rounding a bend you come upon a spring bubbling up at the base of the cliffs. The water has formed a natural basin the size of a bathtub, and you kneel down to splash fresh spring water on your face. As you dip your hands in the basin, you notice that the slick greenish bottom is made of clay.

A natural clay bath is just what you need. Taking off your clothes, you lie down in it. The clay feels slick against your skin. It oozes between your toes and fingers. When you move, it makes a sucking sound. Let yourself sink deeper and deeper into the cool clay until only your nose is sticking out.

The clay surrounds your body soothingly. It feels soft. Smooth. Let the clay draw all the tension out of your body, from your legs, stomach, chest, back, shoulders, arms, hands, and neck. Pain and tension disappear from your head, especially your temples, eyes, and jaw.

Any physical toxins that have accumulated either through poor diet, substance abuse, exposure to chemicals, etc., are pulled out of your body by the clay. Any emotional or mental toxins caused by the residue of heartache, fear, or worry, are likewise drawn out.

When you feel as if the clay has drawn out all physical, emotional, and mental toxins and tension, stand up. The clay molds thickly to your skin, heavy with the toxins and tension it has absorbed. It begins to harden around you like a crust. As it hardens, it gently but firmly reshapes you. It erases worry lines. It straightens stooped shoulders. It lifts and tightens.

When the clay has done its job, head for the sea. You can only take small steps because the crust of clay around you is so thick and hard. Your arms stick out stiffly from your sides.

Reaching the sea, the warm turquoise water washes away the clay from your feet and legs. Wade out until you're standing in water up to your neck. The gentle motion of the water dissolves the clay crust from your entire body. Check your belly button and under your fingernails—yup, clean as a whistle. Free of tension and toxins, you swim as gracefully and playfully as a dolphin, even if you never swam before.

A little way up the beach you see a waterfall. Leaving the sea you follow a path of wide stone steps to the waterfall. Standing under the merrily splashing water, you feel totally refreshed. The water is cool and invigorating. It rains down gently on your head, splashing your face like a tonic. It sluices over your shoulders, down your back and chest. Rivulets of water tickle your legs.

The sun shines through the curtain of water, making the drops sing with light. You whistle a happy tune, or hum snatches of your favorite song. You feel loose and light. Turning your face upward, you let the sweet water splash into your mouth.

Step out from under the waterfall into the warmth of the sun. Squeeze the water out of your hair, which is so clean it squeaks. Your skin feels like silk. All toxins and tension have completely disappeared.

As soon as the sun and the breeze dry you, put on the new clothes you find lying on a rock by the waterfall. They fit perfectly, and show off your new shape to advantage. Fully relaxed, you glow with health and vitality from head to toe, inside and out. It feels great to be in such great shape!

25

WISHING WELL

Do you find yourself sitting around saying, "I wish I could _____,"
or "I wish I had _____," or "I wish I were _____"? Here's your chance
to define those wishes and make them real.

Picture, or sense, yourself on a moss-covered path in a forest.
Afternoon light shimmers through the branches, turning the leaves
a rich green and dappling the path. The energy of aliveness and
growth is all around you.

The path curves to the right and then slants uphill to a grassy
knoll. At the crest of the knoll is a wishing well made of stone. A
brass plaque is inscribed with the words *Wishing Well*, and above the
words is your name. You smile.

Reaching into your pocket you find three gold coins. You hold
them in the palm of your hand, feeling their coolness and their
weight. You examine the first coin. On one side, in raised letters, is a
single word that embodies the essence of one of your wishes. Maybe
you wish you could buy a new house. See the word *Home* centered
on the coin. Encircling it is a garland of intertwined *yes*es. Turning
the coin over you discover a picture of your ideal house done in bas-
relief, with a halo of light around it.

Rub the raised surfaces of the word and the picture between
your fingers. As you rub the coin, picture yourself in your new
home. Happy feelings come alive within you.

When you're feeling so glad you think you might burst, drop the
coin into the well. It flips over and over as it falls, and then
disappears into the depths of the well. After a few seconds you hear
a muffled "plop" as the coin hits the water far below. Your wish has
been received.

Do the same thing with the two remaining coins. If you wish you
were better at generating original ideas, see the word *Creative* on one
side, encircled with *yes*es, and maybe on the other side a picture of
you with a light bulb shining over your head. Rub the surfaces of the

coin and drop it into the well, listening for the sound of it hitting the water. Do the same with the third coin.

After you've made your three wishes, and heard them fall into the water deep in the well, know that your wishes will come true. Believe in them! Look forward to them!

All this wishing has made you thirsty. You notice a wooden bucket tied to a rope that is wound around a winch. You grab the winch handle and turn, lowering the empty bucket. It hits the water with a satisfying splash, and you unwind it a little more to let it fill with water.

As you hoist up the bucket, it is so heavy with water that you have to grab the winch handle with both hands. Up it comes, until you can pull the bucket over to rest on the edge of the well.

You drink the clear, sweet well water, a toast to wishes coming true. The water satisfies not only your physical thirst, but your mental and emotional thirst as well. This is how clear and sweet your wishes are, and how satisfying it is to have your wishes come true. You have wished well, indeed!

26

KARMA KLEANERS

Life has been rough lately, and you just can't seem to do things right. Pressure has come from all sides, putting your self-image through the wringer. It seems as if you've lived five of your worst lifetimes just in the last year, making you feel lower than a snake's belly slithering through mud.

Your poor old self-image is anything but clean and bright. The pressures of life have worn it to tatters. Heartbreak has torn holes in it. It's stained with mistakes. Tears of grief and frustration have shrunk it so that now it's too tight. Anger has popped off buttons. The zipper is stuck, causing your image to hang lopsidedly, gaping where it should be closed.

What do you do? Toss it out and get a new one? You could, but you like the unique material and design of your image. If only you could take it somewhere to have it cleaned and repaired!

Take heart—you can take it to Karma Kleaners. They specialize in image cleaning and alterations. Karma Kleaners is just a short distance from where you live. You see the Karma Kleaners sign proclaiming their slogan: "We alter images of the past to fit the future. No image too dirty to make bright; no image too torn to make right."

A sign in the window says: "Service While You Wait." That's for you. The interior is bright and bustling with activity. Who's behind the counter? A man or a woman? Young or old? He or she smiles and asks if you need help. You sure do. "My image needs a good cleaning," you say, pointing to the stains. "And see, it's got a hole in the back, and another one here, and the zipper is stuck." Your voice trails off, because you're so disheartened by the poor shape your image is in.

The person behind the counter smiles at you understandingly. "No problem at all. We'll have it fixed and cleaned in a jiffy." The cleaner leads you to a dressing room, closing the curtain behind you.

It takes a bit of wiggling to get out of your old image, and lying there in a heap it looks like a sorry mess. You slip on a soft white robe you find hanging on a hook.

The karma cleaner takes your tattered, limp image, holding it as if it were rare and valuable, and hands it to a leprechaun who sits cross-legged, surrounded by spools of thread of every conceivable color and hue. The cleaner explains, "He's our tailor, the best there is at repairing karma." The karma cleaner takes you to a waiting area.

In no time at all the karma cleaner brings you your clean and altered image, hanging on a hanger. Even through the plastic covering you can see how it sparkles and shines. You tear off the plastic and discover that it looks even better than you thought it would. All the stains are gone; all tears have been mended. The color and design of the material are vivid. And no longer is your image of indeterminate shape; it's crisply defined with the necessary amount of starch.

Eagerly, you slip your image off the hanger and put it on. You push your head into the head part, and make sure that all your fingers and toes are on smoothly. It fits perfectly. It gives you room to breathe, but it's been tailored to show you off to advantage. Buttons have been replaced. The zipper glides smoothly and is self-mending.

Look in the mirror, turning to see all sides of yourself. Yes, indeed, you *like* what you see. This sparkling, bright, stylish image is just what you needed. You know that seeing yourself in such a flattering way is going to have a positive effect on how others see you.

Anytime your image becomes dingy or torn, take it to Karma Kleaners. They're open twenty-four hours a day and are there to serve you. A bright image brightens you, which brightens your life.

27

CHARMED

Have you been leading a charmed life? Protected from mishaps? Everything falling smoothly into place? No? Would you like to? Here's help.

With your mind's eye picture, or sense, yourself at the base of a mountain. The mountain is covered with green fields dotted with wildflowers, but the top is covered in mist. A gently sloping dirt path winds back and forth across the mountainside, leading upward.

As you set foot on the path you spy a knapsack. Picking it up, you look inside to find it filled with your favorite food, a jug of fresh water, and your warmest sweater.

Slinging the knapsack on your back you begin to traverse the mountain. The going is easy and breezy under a warm sun. A sweet scent rises from the earth. As you climb you pick flowers: red ones, orange ones, yellow ones.

You make good progress, and, looking back, you see that you're halfway to the top. Sit down to enjoy a bite of food and some water, and then continue on. The path is bordered by bushes with graceful green leaves, and you pick a couple of branches to add to your bouquet.

Along a curve to the left are rows of bluebells; you pick some. Farther along, the path winds to the right and you come upon a cluster of lavender flowers, which you gather with care. You're almost at the top of the mountain. The sun has burned off the mist, and the peak of the mountain rises gloriously against a bright blue sky. It's turned cool, so you put on your sweater.

Just two more quick turns in the path—one to the left, one to the right—bring you to the top of the mountain. And there, in the midst of a field of delicate white lilies-of-the-valley, are an old man and an old woman. They're wearing loose-fitting robes and are sitting on a bench formed by flat rocks. Their hair is as white as the lilies. Wisdom lights their eyes and kindness shapes their mouths.

The old man and the old woman beckon you. You pick some lilies-of-the-valley and offer them your bouquet of rainbow-colored flowers. With pleased smiles, they accept your bouquet.

They, too, have a gift for you. The old man and the old woman hold out their hands to you. Lying in the center of each one's palm is a golden charm that gleams in the rays of the sun.

The charm the old woman offers you is symbolic of an inner quality you want to have, such as strength, insight, creativity, confidence, integrity, etc. You take the charm from the wise old woman's palm and hold it in your left hand.

The charm offered by the old man represents something you want to achieve: love, money, a new home, a promotion, etc. You take the charm from the kind old man and hold it in your right hand.

The charms begin to vibrate in your hands, sending energy rushing up each arm to meet in your heart. You feel strong and calm. From your heart, energy shoots up into your mind, empowering you with insight and knowing. You feel confident about yourself and optimistic about the future. You visualize yourself leading a charmed life, protected from mishaps, with things falling smoothly into place.

Filled with gratitude, you thank the wise old woman and the kind old man for their loving gifts. By visualizing the two golden lucky charms, and feeling the power of their energy uniting within you, you are charmed.

28

SHOUT IT OUT

Welcome to Name Your Nemesis, the mind game everybody can win. Unless you've already achieved total enlightenment, you probably have a nemesis, a pesky negative attitude or behavior that prevents you from achieving greater happiness and success. This inner bugaboo can be the bane of your existence, constantly throwing a wrench in the works. Here's a way to get rid of your particular nemesis.

First, think of a word that captures the essence of your nemesis. Maybe the word is *failure, confusion, hate, laziness, fear, pessimism, craving, inadequacy, procrastination, scarcity*, etc. See or sense the word scrawled on a raggedy piece of gray cardboard.

A creature is holding the cardboard with the word written on it. What does the creature look like? Short and squat? Green and scaly, or pink and hairless? Furry? Does it have claws and pointy ears? What color are its eyes? What shape is its mouth? How is it fixed for teeth? Does it stink? This is your nemesis.

Using your mental voice, say *"No"* to this ugly creature and the negative word it clutches. The creature blinks at you uncomprehendingly. C'mon now, that was pretty feeble. Say *"No"* as if you really mean it! Your nemesis doesn't even budge.

This is going to take real determination. Say *"No"* again, loudly and forcefully. At last, the ugly creature moves back. *Shout* the word *no*. The ugly creature begins to shrink; the ugly word it's holding begins to blur. With all your power, yell *"No"* at this enemy, this saboteur that keeps you from being all that you can be. Your nemesis and its word begin to disintegrate.

Feel how angry you are that this little monster has kept you from having what you want. Shout *"No"* with feeling, refusing to have it in your life! Shout *"No! No! No!"* It crumples into a limp heap. Blast it with *no*'s until your nemesis is pulverized into a mound of dust. A final, long, loud *"No-o-o-o-o-o-o"* blows the dust away.

Slap your hands against each other the way you do when you've just completed a job well done. Now, think of a word that's the opposite of the one you just demolished: *success, clarity, love, vigor, optimism, control, abundance,* etc. This time the word is painted on canvas in a beautiful frame, like a valuable work of art. The letters are large and vibrant. Maybe your first name is intertwined with the power word, or a picture of you smiling peeks out from inside one of the letters.

Holding the word is a wondrous being, the complete opposite of the one you just destroyed. It might be a powerful and graceful animal like a lion, or a magical creature such as a unicorn, an elf, or a genii. It might be your fairy godmother, or a knight in shining armor. This is your ally in success.

This creature is far more beautiful to behold than your nemesis was ugly. It is so alive with positive energy that you can feel its inherent goodness reach out and touch you. You know that this creature has only your best interests at heart. It will help you gain your most heartfelt desires, and protect you from your nemesis.

Say "*Yes*" to it. Your first yes is hesitant and your loving ally stays at a distance. Say "*Yes*" again, putting energy into it. The creature comes closer. Pull positive energy up through the soles of your feet, all the way up through your body, until it shoots out your mouth in a grand and glorious "*Yes!*" The creature glides quickly toward you. Say, "*Yes,* I welcome you!" Say, "*Yes,* I want success and happiness!" The handsome, beautiful creature surrounds you in a radiant, loving glow.

If you see that your nemesis is getting between you and success, or you and happiness, shout it out with "*No.*" Then picture your positive power word and your loving ally bringing happiness and success to you. *Yes! Yes! Yes!*

29

GIFTED

Are you better at giving than receiving? You're not alone. You'd think that knowing how to receive would be a piece of cake, an instinctive ability, but many people find it difficult. Being resistant to receiving has to do with conditioning, control, vulnerability, and fear of obligation.

Maybe you weren't given to as a child, and so you didn't get to practice. Or you might be more comfortable when you're in charge of what's happening: what to give, whom to give it to, and how and when to give it. When you're receiving, you feel vulnerable because it's the other person's show; they're in control. And, of course, in order to receive, you have to be open; that gift from Santa can't get down the chimney with a closed flue. Being open can be scary. And sometimes you resist receiving because you don't want to feel obligated to the giver.

Here's a way to practice receiving in order to accustom yourself to it. Once you can see yourself as a person who receives easily and plentifully, you'll *be* a person who receives easily—and plenty happily. It's a talent worth developing.

Picture yourself sitting in your living room in your favorite chair. Focus on specific details about your living room so you really feel you are there. There's a knock on your door. A voice says, "Package for (your name)." It isn't your birthday or a special holiday, and you haven't ordered anything, so you wonder what it could be.

How do you react? Are you suspicious or expectant? Do you tell the delivery person to go away or do you open the door? Or does it just seem like too much trouble to say or do anything, and so, not hearing a response, the delivery person goes away?

Be aware of whatever resistance you have to receiving the package, but don't act on it. Instead, see yourself going to your front door and opening it wide. A smiling delivery person is holding a gift-wrapped package. If you believe that big things come in small packages, see the package as small. If you believe that big things come in big packages, see it as large.

Sign for the package and thank the delivery person. Taking it inside you open the attached card. It's from someone very dear to you. Eagerly you untie the ribbon and tear off the paper. Opening the box and folding back the tissue paper, you see the very thing you've been wanting. You lift it out of the box, holding it up to the light to admire it. You're thrilled to have received this present, and your heart fills with gratitude. You telephone the person who gave it to you to thank him or her.

Hey, this was pretty easy. You opened the door, received a package, opened the package, and felt warmly and comfortably thankful. With a little practice you just might get the hang of this receiving business.

Think of someone else you'd like to receive a present from and picture him or her knocking at your door, gift in hand. Think of all the people—past, present, and future—you'd like to receive gifts from, including Santa Claus, the Easter Bunny, and the Tooth Fairy. They show up at your door throughout the day, all bearing gifts. Or maybe they all show up at once and you're inundated with brightly wrapped gifts. The gifts come in all shapes and sizes. Some are things you hoped for, others are things you didn't know you wanted until you received them.

By the end of the day your living room is festooned with ribbons and wrapping paper of every hue. You sit in your favorite chair surrounded by piles of gifts, lovingly given and lovingly received. Feel the warm inner glow that comes from allowing yourself to receive. You are truly gifted.

30

RISE AND SHINE

If you were involved in a relationship with someone who repeatedly took, giving back very little; who rarely said thank you; and who physically abused you, how would it affect you? Would it make you angry? Sad? Frustrated? All of the above? At the very least it would make you feel bad about yourself, gradually impairing your self-image. How long would you put up with that kind of unkind behavior? Until it killed you?

Think of the planet Earth as a person who has endured that kind of unloving, unhealthy, unfulfilling relationship with most of its inhabitants. In the last two hundred years, since the beginning of the Industrial Revolution in the late 1700s, when the plundering of the earth's resources escalated, the relationship has deteriorated severely.

Visualize the earth in the beginning of its relationship with humankind as a young maiden, innocent and beautiful, offering love in thousands of different ways. As Earth Mother she was prepared to nurture and support us, and inspire us, unconditionally and indefinitely. But we took her for granted and didn't treat her with respect.

Now the earth seems to be saying, "Enough is enough. Treat me with kindness and respect or this relationship is over!" She's lashing out with angry storms and fires. She quakes and erupts with inner turmoil. Wounds are becoming infected. Illnesses are worsening.

The moment you were born you entered into a relationship with the earth. Her air gave you the breath of life—and still does. Her bounty sustained you—and sustains you still. Use this visualization to establish a loving relationship with the earth, or to enhance the one you already have.

Picture the earth in whatever form it is comfortable for you to speak to. As a maiden, or mother, or even grandmother. As a blue-green photo taken from out in space. As a classroom globe. Or as a sphere of rotating light.

Talk to the earth as you would to someone you care for but have neglected. Talk to her in a way that will make her feel good about herself and increase her self-esteem. Touch her gently from time to time as you speak.

Tell the earth how much you value her bounty and her beauty. Be specific, mentioning particular ways in which she has helped and inspired you. Tell the earth how much she means to you, and that you can't live without her.

Own up to the ways in which you might not have treated her well in the past and apologize for any harm you've caused. Ask for forgiveness. Promise to help the earth in the future, and to appreciate what she does for you. Ask the earth if there's anything in particular that you can do to make her feel better, and to help heal the harm that has been done to her.

As you talk to the earth, you feel a loosening of tension, a dropping away of pain and illness, a shift towards a positive attitude. It's as if that churning in her stomach ceases, the headache goes away, her shoulders straighten, the gleam returns to her eye, the blush to her cheek. Your kind words and sincerity make the earth come alive. Like the legendary phoenix bird, the earth rises from the gray ashes of her old image, and shines radiantly in her new image.

Make a commitment to yourself and to the earth to help her grow through love instead of pain. By holding an image in your mind of the earth being healthy, happy, wealthy, and wise, you help the earth hold the same image of herself. Picture the planet Earth being bountiful and beautiful, with sparkling clear waters, clean and vibrant air, fertile and productive land, and plentiful, verdant forests. Imagine that all beings who dwell on the earth are likewise healthy, happy, wealthy, and wise.

Rise and shine!

PROBLEM SOLVING

31
PLACE OF POWER

Are you being buffeted by the storms of life? Drained by life's demands? Wouldn't it be a relief to have a place to go where you could feel safe? Somewhere to regroup and recharge. To solve problems. A refuge.

Create such a place within you using both your heart and your mind. Even if you already have a physical place on earth that is life-affirming, its merits will be enhanced by having an inner place of power.

Choices of locale are limited only by your imagination, so set your mind free to explore. Take a long deep breath, exhaling slowly, languidly. Then begin your search for a place of harmony and beauty. A place where you can let down your guard and feel safe doing so. A place that infuses you with energy. A place that inspires you.

What place would provide these qualities? Picture various environments and see where your heart wants to take you. A mountaintop? The seashore? A meadow? A cave? A desert? A garden? A forest? A lagoon? A sphere of light? Which environment gives you a warm inner glow, as if a light were switched on inside you?

Whatever the environment, at the speed of thought you're there. Feel the surface beneath your feet. Is it hard or soft? Smooth or crunchy? Take in the details of your surroundings. What's the view from your mountaintop? Is the sea blue or green? What blooms in your meadow? Do cliffs rise from the beach? Do crystal stalactites grow from the ceiling of your cave? Is the forest floor carpeted with moss, pine needles, or leaves? What exotic foliage surrounds your lagoon? Does your sphere of light float in starlit space, or is it suspended in a turquoise sea?

Once you've chosen your place of power, stand in the middle of it and breathe in its energy. Explore it, bringing more and more details into focus. It's your special place, so create it *exactly* the way you want it. Don't skimp!

This being your place of power, whatever you want and need pops into the picture at the speed of thought. Need a place to sit? *Pop!* You've got a rocking chair, or a hammock, or a throne. Need help? *Pop!* Someone's there. Want music? *Pop!* Out of the ethers comes music that calms and inspires. Want something to help you focus on what you want? *Pop!* A movie screen appears so you can project pictures of what you want onto it. Find that you need more space? *Pop!* Instant expansion. Seeking information? *Pop!* A complete book or computer library is at your disposal.

Your place of power is just that. A place where the powers of your mind, heart, and spirit combine to make your wishes come true. It's easy and fun. All you have to do is know what you need or want, picture or sense it, and it appears. To remind yourself, create a sign in your place of power:

THERE ARE NO LIMITATIONS TO
WHAT I CAN CREATE

Once you've visited your place of power several times, it will come easily to mind. Then, whenever you need an environment to help you relax, renew, recharge, heal, solve problems, create, etc., go to your place of power. Doing other visualizations in your place of power will give them added zip. As you become adept at creating what you want in your mental world, you'll become more adept at creating what you want in your physical world. Here's more power to you!

32

MASTER KEY

Wouldn't it be handy to have a master key that could unlock *everything*? That could unlock the doors to success, relationships, wealth, health, wisdom, the past, the future, hearts, minds. Prepare to receive your master key to life.

Imagine that you're standing on a platform facing a crowd of people, most of whom you know, and some you don't. Standing to your right is a man who looks like an elder statesman. His presence is commanding; his face is lined with compassion. His blue eyes sparkle like nuggets of sky beneath clouds of white hair. He could be wearing a business suit, or flowing robes.

In his hands he holds a large, official-looking key. Of what material is it made? Is it ornate or simple? Old-fashioned like a skeleton key, or new?

The distinguished gentleman turns to you and says, "It is my profound pleasure to present you, (your name), with the official key to life. Please accept it with congratulations and best wishes. Use this key to unlock whatsoever is closed to you." He hands you the key and a booklet entitled *Official Key to Life Manual: 1001 Uses*. The crowd of well-wishers breaks into enthusiastic applause, cheering and whistling.

You receive the key gladly, holding it firmly. Feel the weight of it, and the cool smoothness of the metal against your palms. You notice that your name is engraved on the shaft of the key in elegant letters. The key radiates the same forceful presence as the elder statesman.

You leave the platform to thunderous applause. As you descend the platform steps, your sense of anticipation builds. You hurry excitedly to your place of power—the place on earth or in your mindscape where you feel most alive.

Once there, sit down, laying the key in your lap. Although you're not usually one to read instructions, this time you do. The

Official Key to Life Manual: 1001 Uses suggests that you keep this key with you at all times. It explains that the key has two unique properties: (1) It automatically changes size to fit any sized problem, large or small; and (2) It immediately unlocks any kind of problem, so that no lock remains closed to it.

The manual lists the ways in which your key to life can be used. Here are a few of them:

• For problems in general—people, things, situations, attitudes, etc.—picture something that symbolizes the problem. See the problem chained and locked with a padlock, then insert your key into the padlock and turn. Hear a click as the padlock springs open and the chains fall away.

• To unlock success, picture a closed door marked "Success." Fit your key in the lock and turn. The door swings open and someone or something that represents success emerges.

• To unlock love, picture a heart that has been abandoned. Maybe it's boarded up and dark. The lock is rusty, but your key unlocks it. Love and light spill out.

• To unlock knowledge, picture books or computer discs that contain the answers you seek locked behind glass cabinet doors. Your key unlocks their knowledge.

• To unlock wealth, picture a large bank safety deposit drawer. Your key unlocks it, revealing bundles of $100 bills, stacks of rare gold and silver coins, and precious gems.

• To unlock relationships, picture the person with whom you're in conflict locked in a prison cell. Your key sets them free.

These are a few ways to use your key to life to unlock problems, large and small. You'll think of many other uses, or you can refer to the manual. Carry your key with you—put it on your key chain or on a chain around your neck—and use it anytime you have a problem of any kind. Your master key can help set you free.

33

IMAGINING

Has your imagination taken a hike? Or boarded a bus to somewhere else? Whether you're a hod carrier, a doctor, or a musician, imagination is as essential as air and water.

Through imagination we can find the solutions to problems. It breaks down the barriers of space and time, allowing us to roam freely through the past, present, and future. It gives us insight into ourselves and others, inspiring us to reach a little higher. It provides a language in which to dream, and to communicate with our subconscious and our higher consciousness. It's a playground for our minds. Even birds don't always fly to get from A to B; they often fly just for fun. So take your mind off the straight track for a moment, and let it soar.

Where does your instinct tell you to look for your imagination? Did it indeed take a hike up a mountain or deep into a forest? Hike after it. Board the next bus to somewhere else and look up your imagination; it's in a phone book under the I's: "Imagination, (your name)." Or did you stuff your imagination in a box and put it away with your toys when you outgrew them? Have you locked it in a prison, barred from thought?

Track down your imagination, wherever it's gone. See or sense yourself climbing a mountain, or walking on a path of pine needles deep in a forest. Open up that toy chest in the attic. Find the key to your imagination and set it free.

What does your imagination look like? A sphere of spiraling rainbow lights? A wizard with a long white beard? A little girl in a party dress? A sylph? A sprite? Someone from an ancient and mysterious culture? A white dove? A sparkler? A fairy godmother complete with a magic wand of inspiration? Someone well known in your field of interest? Use your imagination!

Introduce yourself and ask if there's a special name your imagination would like to be called. Tell it how glad you are to see it.

Tell it how handsome and beautiful it looks. Thank it for being there. Maybe you bake it a cake or give it a bouquet of flowers.

Your imagination responds warmly and asks what it can help you with. You tell it about a particular problem that you would like to resolve. It listens attentively and agrees to help.

Your imagination takes your hand, or enfolds you in a whorl of light, or puts you on a magic carpet, and off you go on a wondrous journey of play and discovery. You slide down flower petals and cartwheel through star clusters. You rest on high-flying clouds, listening to the universe breathe. You swim with dolphins and soar with eagles. Use your imagination.

The more you set your imagination free to play, the happier you feel. In rediscovering your imagination, you uncover a cache of mental riches. The possibilities are unlimited. Delight spirals around you and within you, creating a vortex of joy.

Then suddenly, in the midst of play, the solution to your problem pops into your mind. It feels as natural, and right, and obvious as the sun coming up in the morning. The solution is so delightfully obvious that it makes you laugh.

Grinning happily from ear to ear, you thank your imagination with all your heart. It tells you that the experience has been a pleasure, and invites you to call on it as often as you want. For problems, and for play, your imagination is here to stay.

34

CUTTING TIES THAT BIND

There are ties that bind, and then there are ties that *really* bind. The positive connections you form with people—love, joy, respect, intimacy, trust—bind in a healthy way. The negative ties—anger, sorrow, hurt, resentment, betrayal—are the ones that *really* bind because they're restricting rather than liberating, contracting rather than expanding. Every negative connection saps your energy, and the more there are, the more emotionally snarled and tense you become. Here's an easy, painless way to unbind yourself.

Imagine that you're standing barefoot on the earth. You might be on soft, warm dirt in the middle of a garden blooming with bright flowers. Or standing with your toes dug into the sand along the water's edge. Or on firm ground in a clearing in a forest. The sky overhead is a weatherman's dream, clear and sunny as far as you can see.

Sprouting from your body in all directions are lines or cords. You might see, or sense, them as telephone lines, or ropes, or hoses. Some might be as thick as a bundle of transoceanic fiber optics, others as thin as string. Some are flexible, glowing with light; others are dark and stiff.

Each line or cord represents a connection you have with someone. The stronger the connection, the thicker the cord. The livelier and healthier the bond, the brighter it glows. The ones that are muddy or black symbolize connections that are unloving and unhealthy, with no life flowing through them.

Your subconscious may or may not show you which cord is connected with which person. You may see, or sense, a person at the end of a cord, or it might simply disappear into space.

Certain areas of your body that have strong emotional attachments, such as your chest, abdomen, and back, might sprout thick clusters of cords. The dark ones are negative connections that have caused you heartache, or that you couldn't stomach, or that have weighed heavily upon you. If a particular part of your body causes you chronic trouble, check to see if you have a negative connection with someone that relates to that area.

The dark, stiff cords are the ones you want to cut loose. They're the ones that drain you of energy and keep you tense. What do you want to cut them with? A sturdy pair of golden scissors? A well-honed knife? A silver dagger? A razor-sharp sword? Choose whatever feels most powerful to you. Heft it in your hand. Feel the coolness and weight of the metal.

Don't worry about cutting a healthy connection by mistake. Whatever cutting instrument you choose has the wondrous quality of only being able to cut through the negative cords—it leaves the healthy cords intact. Best of all, there's gain without pain.

Cut the dark, unhealthy cords one by one, or slice through several at a time. You might feel a slight pressure of resistance as you begin to cut the ties that bind, but no matter how thick the cords are, they are easily severed. The end that is attached to someone else whips away into space. The end attached to you atrophies and dries to dust in a couple of seconds. It crumbles away painlessly, leaving no mark or scar.

As each black cord is severed and falls away, you feel noticeably lighter. Lighter as in *buoyant*. Lighter as in *glowing*. Lighter as in *cheerful*. No longer bound by ties that bind and drain energy, you are free to enjoy all the loving ties that make you feel glad to be alive.

35

LIGHTEN UP

Do the problems of life weigh heavily upon you? Do you feel as if you're carrying the weight of the world on your shoulders? If your problems are getting you down, here are some ways to lighten up.

First, form a picture of what your problems look like and how much they weigh by giving them shape and size. How high are your problems? How wide? How deep? Do you have one big, heavy problem, like a one-ton block of stone? Or do you have several smaller problems stacked up like sacks of cement? (And watch out if the cement should mix with the water of emotions!)

What color are your problems? Gray? Brown? Or black? Are they hard like a rock, shifting like sand, or gummy like tar? Do they give off an odor? Are they hot or cold?

How does the weight of your problems affect you? Does a heavy stone push down on top of your head, giving you headaches? Or put pressure on your neck and back, giving you neck aches and backaches? Do you walk stooped over?

Are problems piled in front of you like a rock wall that you're constantly pushing against? Or do you lug problems behind you in a sack filled with cinder blocks and bowling balls? Either way, problems use up energy and tire you out.

Once you have a concrete picture, or sense, of your problems, you can deal with them more effectively. By lightening your problems in your mind, you help lighten them in your life, so set your imagination free. Here are some lighthearted possibilities.

Imagine that the weight on your head or your shoulders becomes lighter. As it becomes lighter in weight, it also becomes lighter in color. Feel it lifting. Watch it float up into the sky like a cloud and sail out of sight.

You find a hammer and chisel by your feet and chisel your problems down to nothing.

If your problems are stacked up like sacks of cement, take out a penknife and slash a hole in each bag. The problems trickle out steadily and are blown away by the wind.

Need help solving your problems? Call in Mr. or Ms. Problem Solver. It could be anybody you know or have known whom you respect. It could be a wise old man or a faerie queen. Your Problem Solver might wave a magic wand and make your problems disappear. Or whisper the solution into your ear. Or give you a folded piece of paper with something written on it: a word or a diagram. Or hand you the key to your problems. Maybe he or she helps you dump your problems into the dumpster, then drives the garbage truck that hauls them away.

A weight has been lifted! As you change your problems from heavy to light, and from dark to bright, *you* feel lighter and brighter. By taking positive action in your mind, and seeing and feeling the positive changes, you'll be better able to take positive action in your physical life. You'll find that more solutions will present themselves.

Anytime your problems get so big and heavy that they weigh you down, take a moment to lighten up.

36

RIGHT ROAD

Is the road of life sometimes bumpy, causing you to take a few too many detours? Have you gotten so far off track that even NASA couldn't get you home? Use this visualization to help you get back on track, and make improvements to the road so that it's easier to follow.

Imagine that you're outdoors on an overcast day, wandering aimlessly. You wander to the left, you wander to the right. The landscape looks pretty desolate. Suddenly, you notice a large sign. Printed on it in bold, bright letters, are the words: "(your name) Road." Above the sign a flashing neon arrow indicates the direction.

Walking a short distance in the direction indicated, you come to another sign that proclaims: "(your name) Road." What does your road through life look like? Is it narrow or wide? What kind of surface does it have? Asphalt? Dirt? Gravel? Brick? Does the road climb up and down hills, or is it level? Does it wind back and forth, or is it straight?

Let the images of the road surface honestly in your mindscape. What you notice regarding the shape and condition of your road can give you valuable information about whether you tend to make life easy or difficult. After you've seen the road the way it is, re-create it the way you want it to be. Widen the road and make it easy to walk on. If there are potholes, fill them in. If there are rocks in the way, remove them.

Resurface your road with whatever material would be most comfortable to walk on. It could be firm but yielding like a composition tennis court, or made of wood like a basketball court. It could be good old organic earth. Pave it with gold. Sprinkle it with rose petals. How about a yellow brick road?

Recontour your road. If you're worn out from climbing too many hills, level them. Does your road wind back and forth, confusing you? Straighten it.

What about the borders alongside the road? Are they barren and brown, or verdant and green? Landscape your road so it looks inviting. Plant bushes and colorful flowers. Add graceful shade trees, and maybe some fruit trees so you can stop and snack when you get hungry.

And how are you fixed for company? Are you alone? Is that okay, or are you lonely? Is there anyone you'd like to invite along? Do it. See them beside you and feel how glad you are to have their company.

If other people are already with you, check 'em out. Did you invite them, or did they invite themselves? Are they friends or foes? Are they helping you get where you're going, or hindering you? Do they crowd you, or give you plenty of room? Do they let you go at your own pace?

Be aware of who's with you and why. If you see someone you don't like, or who's pushing you off the road, tell them to take a hike. If they're connected to you in some way you can't change, picture them helping you, or at least not interfering. Or see them making progress on their own road.

When you use the power of your mind, there are unlimited solutions. By landscaping your mindscape the way you want, you can create a smoother road through life. The right road can keep you out of left field.

37
IRONING IT OUT

What's life without a few wrinkles? If you're out there living life—not just letting life live you—you'll probably encounter some wrinkles from time to time. If you want to iron them out, here's how.

Picture your life as a large, uniquely designed quilt. You might keep your quilt of life folded up in a closet. Or at the foot of your bed to pull up at night for a comforter to dream under. Or you might hang it on your wall, like a work of art.

Wherever you keep your quilt of life, get it out and take a good look at it. It's covered with different-sized squares in different colors and designs, representing different parts of your life. Stitched around the edge of each square is a name telling which part of your life that square represents.

In no particular order the squares might say: "Love Mate, Job, Bank Account, Home, Mom, Dad, Brother, Sister, Kids, Car, Pets, Knowledge, Sports, Music, School, Diet, Mildred, Fred, Aunt Tillie, Fitness, Reading, Writing, Dancing, Hopes, Ideas, Relaxation, Sleeping, Laughing, Friendship, Health, Hobby."

What's the design of each square? Friendship might be two hands shaking. Diet might be the number of pounds you want to weigh. Bank account: the number of dollars you want to have. Love Mate: a heart shot through with an arrow and stitched with intertwined initials. Ideas: a light bulb with shine lines around it. Sports: a trophy. Well, you get the idea.

Looking at the different squares you notice that some of them lie flat and smooth, while some of them are bunched up and wrinkled. Maybe that square with the car logo is badly wrinkled because you've been having car trouble. Or you've been quarreling with a friend, and the square with that person's name on it is wrinkled. There's no time like the present to smooth out those wrinkles. Get out the iron you keep in the cupboard, or take your quilt of life to Karma Kleaners and have it pressed.

Before ironing, check the square for stains and rips. Put spot remover on the stains and mend any tears. Then press the iron on the square, or put the wrinkled square in the clothes press. Hear the steam puff out the vents. See the mist. Feel that cloud of wet warmth on your face.

Press all the squares that need it, until every wrinkle is ironed out. When you've finished ironing a particular square, run your hand over it. It's smooth, and still warm from the iron. As you iron out the wrinkles in your life, you're flooded with a feeling of deep satisfaction. You feel as warm and smooth as the squares you ironed.

When every wrinkle has been ironed out, admire your quilt of life. Spread it out. Notice how colorful it is, how detailed, how full of life! Even though each square has its own design, each design complements and is in harmony with the others. See how the different parts of your life join together to form a unique whole. See your life as complete and smooth.

Whenever parts of your quilt of life become wrinkled from everyday wear and tear, iron those wrinkles out! Picturing the wrinkles being ironed out gives your subconscious a strong message to get to work solving problems. Doing the weekly ironing will help make life smoother.

38

PUT ON YOUR THINKING CAP

You've been frying your brain cells trying to figure out the solution to a problem. Or you've been wrestling with an idea that keeps slipping out of your mental grasp. And what do you have to show for all that mental effort? Nothing. Nada. Rien. Zero. Zip.

What you need is your thinking cap! But where is the dangnabbit thing? You probably left it where you last did some serious thinking. At the office? Or a friend's? At the gym? In the car? In bed? Wherever you think you left it—go and get it!

Or maybe you put your thinking cap away in the closet. Picture your closet, and look inside. There's your thinking cap hanging neatly on a hook. Or it's on the topmost shelf in a hatbox labeled "Thinking Cap." Or it's fallen on the floor with your shoes. Or it's stuffed away in the very back of the closet.

Take it out and brush it off. What does your thinking cap look like? What color is it? What texture? Do you have one all-purpose thinking cap, or different styles for different problems? What kind of hat fits your style of thinking? What kind would *improve* your style of thinking?

For example, your thinking cap could be a top hat—for when you need to quickly pull out a thought like a rabbit, or think debonair thoughts. It could also be a golden crown, a bowler, a space helmet (for far-out thoughts), a cowboy hat, a straw boater, a turban, an Indian feather headdress, a garden party hat, a sombrero (for learning Spanish), a halo (for angelic thoughts), a watch cap, a diamond tiara, a sunbonnet, a beach hat, a fez, a babushka, etc.

For visualizing yourself playing a particular sport, there's always the appropriate sports headgear: baseball cap, football or motorcycle helmet, golf hat, ski hat, fencing mask, tennis visor, etc.

Let your subconscious show you which thinking cap is best for you. Once you know what your thinking cap looks like, put it on. It settles on your head as if it were custom made for you—and it is!

The weight of it feels comfortable and comforting. You feel relaxed and secure.

As it rests on your head, your thinking cap begins to get warm. When it's all warmed up it makes a sound: a buzz, a hum, a whistle like a tea kettle, an electric crackle. Suddenly your thinking cap lights up like a Christmas tree, or glows like a neon light. Bright and merry, it radiates light into your head. The light is absorbed by your brain, and your brain cells light up. Your mind is sparked into action.

Your mind starts generating ideas. They might come slowly at first and then faster and faster. A sense of excitement builds. Thoughts, ideas, and solutions tumble out of your mind, one after another. Each one is bright and crisp and strong. Let them flow. You're bursting with an abundance of ideas. One idea sparks another—and another—and another. Pick out the brightest ones and write them down so you don't lose them.

Keep your thinking cap on for as long as you need to. If you take it off, make a mental note of where you put it. Then the next time you want to give something some thought, you'll be able to put your mind right on it. Thinking's a snap with your thinking cap.

39
BLOCKBUSTERS

You know what you want and how to get it. You've been moving toward your goal quite nicely, thank you, when suddenly your way is blocked by some tangible or intangible obstacle. A negative attitude, an unforeseen situation, or a saboteur stands between you and what you want.

Clear the way to your goal by busting the block. The beauty of this visualization is that you can bust the block without even knowing exactly what it is or how it got there. Just picture, or sense, a square block in front of you. How high is it? How wide? How deep? What color is it? Go up and touch it. Is it slippery or rough? Hot or cold? What's it made of? Does it have a smell? Does it make a noise? A pop? A wheeze? A rattle? A squeak?

Once you've defined the size and texture of your block, step back from it. Out of your pocket take a silver whistle and give three sharp blasts. Immediately your team of Blockbusters appears in front of you. The word *Blockbusters* is emblazoned on their chests. These guys are bruisers. They're broad and bold, tall and tough. They might be the entire defensive team of the Chicago Bears, a horde of marauding Huns, a SWAT team, a Klingon spaceship crew, or any combination thereof. Whoever they are, they know their business and they mean business.

The Blockbusters have the determination, the strength, the skill, and the equipment to crush anything you tell them to. You give the orders. Another sharp blast on your whistle gets their attention. In a loud, authoritative voice command them, "Bust this block!"

The Blockbusters acknowledge your command with a salute, and begin chanting in unison, "Bust this block! Bust this block! Bust this block!" They start giving the block everything they've got. They slam into it and pummel it. They hit it with sledgehammers. Great chunks of the block break off. Swords slash it. Lasers slice it. The cracks in it widen. Sound shatters it. The block falls apart. Blasters blast it. Before your very eyes the block disintegrates into a pile of rubble and dust.

Another blast of your whistle brings in a construction truck to haul away any remaining debris. In practically no time at all the area where the block stood is completely clear. The Blockbusters line up on either side of you. They've done a tremendous job and you thank them for their efforts. With a final blast on your silver whistle, you dismiss them.

Now you can see your goal! Before, with the block blocking you, you could neither see it nor get to it. With the obstinate obstacle between you and your goal removed, a feeling of excitement surges within you. Your goal glows with an inner light that clearly defines its shape and size. It's just big enough to be challenging, but not so large as to be intimidating: it's just the right size for you. Your goal looks so attractive that it pulls you to it, and simultaneously your sense of excitement propels you forward.

With nothing in your way you move toward your goal, arriving at it smoothly and quickly. Embrace it; it's yours! Enjoy it! Be proud of yourself for busting the block. You're so happy that you feel like one enormous grin.

Your Blockbusters are on call twenty-four hours a day. Anytime you feel blocked—even if you don't know by what—call in your Blockbusters. They're built to bust any block you have, and they mean business.

40

WELL OUT OF IT

Are your spirits in need of a lift? Has life got you down? Well, if you feel like you've hit bottom, the good news is that there's nowhere to go but up.

Imagine yourself at the bottom of a deep, dark well. It has no water, but the floor on which you sit is sweaty with moisture that soaks through your clothes. The air is thick with quiet and darkness. Looking up, all you can see is a tiny circle of light way above you.

What do you do?

Decide whether you want to stay at the bottom of the well or get out. Maybe you feel helpless to do anything about it. Maybe it seems easier to stay at the bottom of the well in the darkness than to face the light. Maybe it even feels safe down there.

Does staying in the well reflect how you deal with problems? Do you tend to let problems get the best of you because solving them seems like too much trouble? Do you defeat yourself from the git-go by saying, "Well, this is hopeless. I couldn't get out of this mess if I tried"?

How does staying at the bottom of the well make you feel? Isolated? Alone? Cut off from family and friends? Shut out of opportunities, fun, and success? Do you feel removed from life?

If you answered yes to any of the above questions, do yourself a favor and decide to get out of the well. Don't let worrying about how you're going to get out prevent you from making the decision. Once you sincerely decide to get out of the well, how to accomplish it will come to you. Solutions are limited only by your imagination.

Imagine water pouring into the well from an underground spring below you. The rising water floats you easily to the top. If you can't swim, you can in the visualization, or you can create a life preserver to keep you afloat.

A covey of fireflies suddenly appears. They illuminate rocks jutting out from the well wall at evenly spaced intervals, or a set of metal rungs, and you use them to climb out.

In your pocket you discover a large balloon and, leaning against the wall, a helium tank. You inflate the balloon, tying it with a shoelace, and it lifts you gently out of the well.

There's nothing wrong with calling for help—loudly and vehemently. A friend or a passing stranger hears you and lowers a rope to haul you out. Or an angel flying by hears you and swoops down on golden wings to carry you up.

A spaceship hovering overhead beams you up in a column of light.

Up and up you go, spirits lifting. Bursting into the sunshine, you squint a bit until your eyes adjust to the bright light. Take a long, deep breath of fresh air. The sound of birds singing is music to your ears. You feel mighty proud of yourself for getting out of the well so well.

Whenever you feel down, stuck at the bottom of a deep, dark well, think of a way to get out. Make it easy. Make it fun. By solving the problem of getting out of the well in your imagination, you'll find it easier to solve problems—and solve them creatively—in your everyday life.

41
STRONG MEDICINE

Sometimes life's problems require strong medicine to heal them. That problem with your mate, or business partner, or checkbook, or health sometimes needs extra power to resolve it. Here's how to make and use strong medicine.

Picture a Native American woman standing in front of you. Her bearing is calm and confident. What is she wearing on her feet? Notice the distinctive beaded design on her ceremonial clothes. Her face is compassionate, but with eyes full of wise secrets. Ask her her name. She is a medicine woman, here to help you gather power items for your medicine pouch.

Facing one another you each raise both hands and hold them palms out toward one another. Taking a step toward each other, you place the palms of your hands together, then lace fingers in greeting.

She says, "Let us begin." From a worn leather pouch worn on a thong under her clothing, she takes a pinch of powder. Rubbing it between her thumb and forefinger, she makes a pattern of lines on your face. As she traces the outlines of your face, you feel opened and protected.

The medicine woman hands you your own medicine pouch, cinched shut. You open it. Inside is a seed that might be a seed of love, of wisdom, of power. You thank her.

To find items of power, the medicine woman takes you to places where the earth's power is especially strong. You collect items that contain the power of the earth, the wind, the sea, and the sun, as well as items that contain or symbolize the power of significant events and people in your life.

These are some of the power items you can put in your medicine pouch: an eagle feather; a bead; a flint; a photo of yourself enjoying a past success; a photo of yourself enjoying a future success; a medal; hair from the mane of a wild horse or a lion; a seashell; a gold coin; a piece of wood from your favorite tree; a tiny carving of an animal made of precious or semi-precious stone, which embodies a trait that you value; the ring of an ancestor; a handful of pollen.

When you have collected all your items of power you will know it by a feeling of completeness. The medicine woman then takes you into a ceremonial teepee with a fire burning in its center. She tells you to pour the contents of your pouch into the hollow of a small rock. To your amazement, all the items you placed in your pouch have turned to powder, swirled with the colors of each object.

The medicine woman takes sacred water from a gourd and sprinkles it over the powder. She chants a song of power, blowing gently on the powder as she sings. She holds the powder up to the fire, and then pours the empowered powder into your pouch. You place the pouch under your clothing.

Once again facing the medicine woman, you each raise your hands, palms toward each other, and clasp them. Your hands tingle and vibrate with the power that passes into them. You give thanks.

The powder in your pouch is strong medicine. Kept with you, it wards off mishap and encourages wisdom. When facing a particularly difficult problem, place a pinch of power powder on a mental picture of the problem. For protection, sprinkle it across entrances of home, meeting places, classrooms, offices, etc. For insight, trace lines on your forehead. For healing, trace lines on the affected area of your body.

Ask the medicine woman for help anytime you need it just by picturing her. From time to time you and she will gather other items of power to add to your pouch. Renewed and replenished, your strong medicine will stay strong, helping you in all ways, and always.

42

DREAM HOUSE

Do you have a dream house?

Where is it located? On top of a rolling green hill? At the edge of a forest? Overlooking a sparkling lake or the sea?

What style of architecture is it? Rustic? Greco-Roman? Ranch? Tudor? Modern? Victorian? Art Deco? Colonial?

Fix the details of your dream house firmly in mind. Is it made of wood, or brick, or cinder blocks? Are there picture windows? Dormer windows? Are there balconies and decks? Is the roof flat or slanted, shingled or tiled? How is it landscaped?

When you've formed a picture, or sense, of your dream house, see a sign at the entrance to the driveway: "(your name) Dream House." Drive up the driveway, get out of the car, and walk up to your front door. What does the door look like? Find the door key on your key chain and open the door.

You enter a foyer containing a small table, a chair, and a coatrack. Leave something of yours in the foyer: a hat, a coat, a scarf, a bag, a pair of gloves.

Excitedly, you walk into the living room. It's decorated exactly the way you dreamed it would be. There's even a framed photo of someone you love on an end table. But wait, there's something peculiar. In the living room is a bed with the covers turned back as if waiting for someone to get into it and go to sleep. There's even a mint wrapped in gold foil on the pillow.

You think it odd to have a bed in a living room, but you're curious and eager to see the rest of the house. Walking into the dining room you find, instead of a dining table, another bed with the covers turned down, with dining chairs around it.

This is getting curiouser and curiouser. You tear through the house; downstairs to the basement, upstairs to the second floor, and up more stairs to the attic. Every room is decorated and furnished exactly the way you dreamed it would be, except that it has a bed with the covers turned down. Naturally the bedroom has a bed, but so does the family room and the library. Even the kitchen and the bathrooms have beds.

What's going on, you wonder? What kind of dream house is this, anyway? It is literally a dream house. A house in which you dream. A dream house you live in while you sleep, to help solve problems and make your dreams come true.

Just as you're ready to fall asleep, imagine driving up the driveway to your dream house. You get out of your car and enter the foyer, where you leave a personal article. Then picture yourself going into the room that best suits your dream needs.

If you want to focus your dreams on a specific problem, go to the appropriate room and get into the bed you find there. If you want to be nourished by a dream, go to the dining room. If you want to cook up an idea, go to the kitchen. If you need information, go to the library. If you need to eliminate something from your life and be cleansed, the bed in the bathroom is the place. If you want to have more family closeness, or to solve a family problem, sleep in the family room. To work out something in your subconscious, go to the basement. For spiritual dreams, sleep on the top floor with the windows open.

By picturing yourself sleeping in a specific room in your dream house, you let your subconscious know what you want to focus on. It might take several nights to get the hang of this, but as you continue to sleep in your dream house you'll see that you *can* affect the direction of your dreams. When you wake up, picture yourself putting on whatever personal article you left in the foyer; this will help you remember what you dreamed. Then get in your car and drive away.

Problems can be solved and dreams come true when you dream in your dream house.

43

MAGIC WAND

Are miracles in short supply? Has the magic gone out of your life? You need your fairy godmother.

"Oh, no, I'm way too old for that kind of silliness. Only children can have a fairy godmother."

Oh, really? Where is it written that no one over twelve is allowed to have a fairy godmother?

It doesn't matter why or when your fairy godmother boarded a bus to somewhere and stayed there, taking her magic wand with her; you can still put the magic back in your life.

Picture yourself calling your fairy godmother on the magic hotline. (Surprise, surprise; you had her number.) She answers on the first ring. And surprise, surprise, again; she remembers you fondly. Those times you got what you wanted—or a surprise treat— that was her doing. She asks how you are. Well, you're fine, except there's no magic in your life. You ask her to please come back.

As fast as you can say "Alakazam-kazoo," your fairy godmother arrives in a swirl of sparkles and pastels. You light up like a Christmas tree at the sight of her. Give her a big hug and tell her how glad you are to see her.

Your fairy godmother hugs you back, kisses you on the forehead, and then whisks out her magic wand. With a twinkle and a twirl she waves her magic wand over your head three times. Magic dust spirals through the air like gold dust, like silver glitter, like tiny stars, and settles on you and makes you shine. Suddenly you feel released, like a balloon floating up into the sky. Laughter bubbles up inside you. You feel sparked with love. Life is filled with promise.

Your fairy godmother says, "Make a wish." You tell her that special something you've been yearning to have, or do, or be. Again she waves her magic wand over your head, sending spirals of stardust cascading over you. You know in your heart, as surely as you breathe, that your wish will come true.

Then your fairy godmother does a most surprising thing: she gives you your own magic wand. It's as light as a feather and fits in your hand as if it were custom made. You thank her for this wondrous gift.

It occurs to you that maybe the difference between having magic in your life as a child, and having it as an adult, is that as an adult you can be in charge of your own magic—with friendly assists from your fairy godmother. As you think this thought, your fairy godmother nods her head at your insight. She promises to be around whenever you need her, but she has given you the power to make your own wishes come true. Best of all, there's no limit on the number of wishes you can make—and make come true.

Everyone can benefit from a little magic, so if you want to, wave your magic wand over relatives and friends. If you have an adversary, sprinkle him or her with magic and transform an enemy into an ally. Wave your magic wand over people you hear about in the news who have had bad news and could use a wish come true. Wave your magic wand over your home, the town you live in, and the planet, to promote peace and prosperity.

Use your magic wand often, for yourself and for others—it won't lose its magic. In fact, the more often you use your magic wand, the more powerful it becomes! So wish away, and make your wishes come true.

44

GIFTING

Have you had a misunderstanding with someone that you'd like to clear up? Or would you just like to be closer? The following imagery will help heal emotional wounds and inspire closeness.

Picture, or sense, your friend as if she were standing in front of you. What kind of shoes does she have on? What is she wearing? How tall is she compared to you? Look closely at your friend's head and face. What color hair does she have? What color skin? Look into her eyes. What color are they? Is there a particular scent that you associate with this person? A particular expression, either facial or verbal?

Once you have a sense of your friend standing in front of you, invite her to sit down and get comfortable. Offer her tea and cake. Begin by telling her what you like about her. Maybe it's her smile and easy humor. Maybe it's her gentleness and strength. As you compliment her you feel yourself fill with warmth and caring.

If there's been a wrinkle in your relationship, tell her that you want to iron it out. Explain how you feel. Ask her how she feels. Apologize for any hurt you might have caused, and tell her how much the friendship means to you.

As a way of showing your friend that you care, give her a gift. As soon as you think "gift," you see a beautifully wrapped box floating in the air in front of you. The box may be large or small, flat or tall. It's wrapped in paper that is your friend's favorite color, and tied with a big, fancy bow. You might already know what's inside, or you might have to wait until your friend opens the box to find out.

Take the beautifully wrapped box in both hands, and present it to your friend. As you hand her your gift, your heart fills with tenderness.

Your friend reaches out to accept your gift, taking it in both hands. Smiling in anticipation, she unties the ribbon and takes off the lid. Tissue paper in pastel hues peeks out of the top of the box. It crinkles and rustles as your friend reaches into the box to lift out the gift.

The gift might be something you know your friend really wants. Or it might be something that is symbolic of your caring, or of a quality you'd like to have in the friendship, such as a brightly glowing ball of light, jewelry in a particular shape, a candle, something heart-shaped, a crystal, or a flowering plant.

Your friend loves the gift and exclaims over it enthusiastically. It's *exactly* what she wanted! Your friend thanks you sincerely, clearly touched by your thoughtfulness. With grins spreading across each of your faces like melting butter, you hug each other warmly. Your friendship is now closer and stronger than ever.

Anytime things aren't going smoothly with someone you care about, or you want to be closer, the gift of giving heals and inspires.

45

DOLPHINS AND EAGLES

You've got a problem. What do you do? Confront it? Ignore it? Stay in bed with the covers pulled over your head? Leap into action? Ask for help?

Although some problems seem to resolve themselves over time, most problems are solved because someone acknowledged that the problem existed and decided to do something about it. All of us on earth are being challenged by some pretty big environmental, political, social, and economic problems; here's a way to open your heart and your mind to solutions.

Most solutions evolve out of the sea of emotions, or fall into consciousness from the sky of the mind, or from a combination of the two. As residents of the sea, dolphins are more efficient in their environment than we are in ours; they may even be smarter than we are. Dolphins are also sophisticated communicators, and have a tradition of helping people in distress.

Picture yourself standing on the shore of any coastline in the world. Feel the sand beneath your feet and the wind blowing on your face. Standing there, you ponder a problem that's been bothering you.

Suddenly, at your feet, you hear a series of clicks. Looking down, you see a dolphin looking up at you, holding the solution to your problem in its beak. You take the solution the dolphin offers. The solution will be in symbolic form. It could be a spiraled nautilus shell that whispers the solution when you hold it to your ear. Or a bottle containing a folded note with the solution written on it. Or a gold doubloon from a sunken treasure, with a raised symbol or word; a fish to nourish you; an anchor to prevent you from being adrift; or a miniature boat to sail in. Whatever the symbol, you immediately understand its significance.

You thank the dolphin for its help, and it makes another series of clicks and squeaks. Using its powerful tail, it jumps gloriously into the air, then dives into the deep out of sight, but not out of mind.

At the same time as you receive the solution to your problem, visualize dolphins in seas all over the world delivering solutions to fishermen, tanker captains, pearl-divers, scuba divers, heads of state, sailors, clam-diggers, swimmers, religious leaders, and marine biologists. Picture people in the seas, and on the seas, and by the seas, gladly receiving solutions from the beaks of dolphins.

Now picture yourself on your favorite piece of earth in the world. You're pondering a problem. High in the sky above, you hear the flutter of powerful wings. Looking up, you see an eagle hovering over your head and looking down at you with his eagle-sharp eyes. In his beak is the symbolic solution to your problem. The eagle drops the solution into your lap. It might be a pair of special eyeglasses that will help you see the solution. Or a glowing light bulb of a bright idea, a miniature plane in which to let your thoughts soar, a cornucopia of abundant ideas, an olive branch for peaceful thoughts, or a star to guide you.

You thank the eagle for your solution. The eagle gives you the eagle eye, then flies in a circle around your head before soaring into the sky and out of sight, but not out of mind.

At the same time, in lands all across the world, eagles deliver solutions to farmers, miners, contractors, heads of state, scientists, gardeners, religious leaders, campers, hunters, bicyclists, cooks, developers, athletes, and parents. Picture people on high land, flat land, low land, hilly land, gladly receiving solutions from the beaks of eagles.

In your mind and in your heart exist innumerable solutions. Let dolphins and eagles be your special allies, bringing solutions to you and others whenever you ask and imagine it so.

MENTAL AND EMOTIONAL HEALTH

46
OPEN MIND

Do you have a closed mind when it comes to your heart? Have your mind and your heart been leading separate lives? If your mind is so closed to emotions that your head rules most of the time, you're missing out.

When thoughts and feelings work together in harmony, a synergy is created: a momentum gathers between heart and mind that allows each to increase the capacities of the other. The result is that the combined energies create greater strength and clarity than either your heart or your mind can produce independently.

Visualize your mind. The picture you see might be an anatomical brain, a sphere of light, a computer, or a quartz crystal. Take a moment to get a feel for your mind. Does it seem bright or dim? Crisp or soggy? Warm or cool?

Then picture, or sense, a hallway leading out from your mind. Is it straight or does it curve? If the hall is dark, turn on a light. If it's narrow, make it wider.

Tell your mind that you'll be back, and then move—walk, float, skip—down the hall until you come to a barrier. What blocks the way might be a closed door, a rusty iron gate, a brick wall, or a floor-to-ceiling jumble of barbed wire and brambles. It might be a bigger-than-life person who glares at you with arms defiantly crossed. Whatever it takes to clear the hall—do it. Unlock the door with the key you find in your pocket. Oil the hinges on the rusty gate and swing it open. Blast away the brick wall with your laser phaser. Call in a crew of strong-armed Blockbusters to clear the barbed wire, or to remove the person in your way.

The hallway is now bright, wide, and clear. You hear a pulsating sound reverberating through the hall; it's so powerful that you can feel the vibrations in your feet. Just ahead glows a warm light that pulsates to the beat of the sound. The closer you get, the brighter the light becomes, and the louder the sound.

This is your heart. You might sense it as an anatomical heart, or as a Valentine heart. However you see it, it's time for a heart-to-heart talk. Tell your heart hello and that you've changed your mind. Explain that you intend to be more open-minded about emotions, and that you've removed the barriers so there can be a free-flowing exchange between heart and mind. Your heart is excited to hear the good news and for a moment beats just a little faster.

As you move back toward your mind, the energy of your heart flows along the hall behind you, filling it with warm light. You come to the place where the barrier was and find that your mind has come to meet your heart halfway, shining with a bright electric light.

Your heart and mind move toward each other, one glowing warmly, one shining brightly. When the two energies meet, they create a synergy of light brighter than either one alone. A gently pulsating light, at once clear and warm. A surge of power flows within you, and you experience a clarity of thought and a strength of emotion you had forgotten you had.

Whenever you feel mentally uptight, remove the barriers and let in your heart. One plus one equals more than two—and feels like a million.

47

CLEAR HEART

How's your love quotient? Up to par? If not, and you want more love in your life, you might want to clear out the old to make room for the new.

Picture your heart as a cozy cabin in the woods, with four rooms or chambers. The cabin sits in the heart of a sunny clearing, surrounded by ivy, ferns, and four-leaf clovers. Beyond the edge of the clearing rises a majestic forest.

Before entering your heart, look to see how the cabin has been cared for. Does the outside seem to be in good repair? Are there flowers? Open the door. Does it need to be oiled? If it's dark, turn on the lights. If there's no electricity, use your bright halogen lantern.

When was the last time you checked to see just who was living in your heart? In the living room you see the figures and faces of people you love and who love you. It gladdens your heart to see them, and you hug one another.

Then check the other rooms in your heart to see who else is there. Are people from the past—people whom you were once emotionally attached to, but who are no longer a constructive part of your life—hiding out? There might be people hiding in your heart whom you used to like or love, but who were unkind to you. They could have become so large with your anger and pain that those you love and who love you are squeezed into corners with no room to move or even breathe.

Kick the unloving people out of your heart. If they resist, whining, "But I like it here. I have nowhere else to go," don't let them manipulate you into feeling sorry for them. Tell them that only those who love you and wish you well are welcome in your heart.

If they still refuse to leave, call for help. Those who love you will be only too glad to help oust misery. Call on them to grab the unloving people, and with you pushing from behind, the unwanted are out the door in no time. Throw their baggage out after them. Tell them not to darken the doorway to your heart again, unless they come in light. Watch them trudge off into the forest, out of sight.

Check the rest of the rooms. Clear out anybody who doesn't have love for you living in *their* hearts. This applies to family members, former romantic partners, friends, acquaintances, business relationships, teachers, etc. Make sure that they take the shadows of their memories with them.

Do a final check of all four rooms of your heart cabin. Okay, how are you fixed for love now? See the figures and faces of those you love and who love you. Do they have enough room? You bet. They have room to breathe and room to dance. A tender love song plays softly, and love light brightens every corner. Birds sing sweetly through the open windows, and a breeze wafts through. Flowers have sprung up around the door to the cabin.

If there's a special someone you would like to invite into your heart, do so now. Put out the welcome mat for him or her. Ask him or her to dance. Don't worry about there not being enough room for all the love you desire; the walls of your heart will expand to give love room to grow, and to let in new love.

Your heart is cleared for love—let it in!

48

NEGAVAC

Have you got those lowdown negativity blues? Is negativity hanging around you in dark clouds of mental dust and emotional dirt? Has it settled in places around your home and where you work? If negativity is clouding your thinking and making you feel lousy, it's time to get out your trusty Negavac.

Negavac is the industrial-strength vacuum cleaner engineered to suck up negativity. This vacuum cleaner is so strong—how strong is it? It could suck paint off aluminum siding, fleas off a dog, the green out of grass. But it's designed to vacuum up only negativity, without harming anything else, and it's so powerful that no negativity can escape it.

Picture the door to the broom closet where you store all your cleaning paraphernalia. Open it. There's your Negavac, light, compact, and ready to go. What shape is it? What color?

The Negavac has some nifty features. The first is that it comes with Mr. and Mrs. Clean; one vacuums and the other shines up after. The nozzle shaft can be extended or retracted to any length so you can reach everywhere. And the Negavac is able to suck up any amount of negativity without getting full, because it's equipped with a conversion generator that instantly converts negative energy to positive. So while you're sucking up negativity with the nozzle, positivity is blowing out of the canister into the air.

Mr. or Mrs. Clean begins by vacuuming the negativity from within and around you, sweeping the nozzle up and down your body from head to toe, front and back. You feel a slight pulling sensation, but it's pleasant. The pain is suctioned from that bad knee of yours; the disappointments from your heart; the ache from your back, neck, or head; the worries from your mind.

Hear the hum of the motor. Hear bits of negativity rattle and snap through the hose, just as if you were vacuuming your carpet. The sound of dirty, dusty negativity being sucked up gives you a feeling of accomplishment and satisfaction. When no more clatter can be heard in the Negavac hose, you know you're clean as a whistle. You sparkle and shine. You feel carefree. Positive.

After you're clean, ask Mr. and Mrs. Clean to clean your home of grimy negativity. There might be specific areas you want to point out. That place in the living room where you had an unpleasant phone conversation. The argument that took place at the kitchen table. The bed where you had a nightmare. And don't worry, Mr. and Mrs. Clean do floors, windows, ceilings, walls—you name it, they clean it!

When all negativity has been suctioned out of your home, send Mr. and Mrs. Clean to whatever areas of your life could stand a good negativity cleaning: car, office, gym, etc. Use the Negavac to clear the air of negativity in a meeting room, before and during a meeting. If you're going to talk with someone with whom you have a conflict, ask Mr. and Mrs. Clean to stand by with the Negavac to keep the conversation flowing positively.

Whenever and wherever you think negativity might be hanging around causing discord or draining energy, get out the Negavac. Suck up negativity and fill your environment with positivity.

49
STRONGBOX

Been feeling a little weak in the willpower department, lately? Or maybe you've had the mental concentration of Swiss cheese? Not up to toting that briefcase or jogging that extra mile? Here's a way to infuse yourself with strength.

Imagine that you're digging in the earth with a shovel. You might be preparing a garden for planting, or digging holes for fence posts. Or maybe you're digging just for the fun of it, to see what you can dig up.

As you dig, feel the wooden handle of the shovel in your hands. Hear the scrunch of the shovel each time it bites into the earth. Smell the rich, loamy odor of the earth.

What are you wearing on your feet? Boots? Loafers? Old running shoes? Or are you barefoot?

You're digging away when suddenly the metal edge of your shovel thwunks against a hard object. Curious, you shovel out more dirt, exposing the corner of a box. Kneeling down, you excitedly scoop earth away with your hands to reveal a metal strongbox. It might be plain or ornate, old or new.

Pulling it free, you lift it out and place it on the ground. On the top is a rectangular gold plate bearing the following inscription:

> What's in this box will make you strong
> For however often, for however long.
> More valuable than gold,
> Into yourself enfold,
> For to (your name) it does belong.

The hasp on the lid is held fast by a padlock. You give it three sharp tugs and it opens. Heart pounding with anticipation, you place your hands on either side of the lid and lift it open. Inside is a dazzling ball of golden-white light. It's the clearest, most radiant light you've ever seen.

The ball of light floats up out of the box and hovers just in front of you at about shoulder height. Free of the strongbox, the ball of light expands and comes alive with thousands of dancing sparks of light. This ball of light represents your strength, your power, your will to act.

Choose an area within you which needs strengthening. It could be that your mind needs strength for concentration, or your throat needs strength for clear expression. Maybe your heart needs strength for emotional peace, or your stomach for digesting something that's happened. On the physical level there might be some part of your body that's been ill, or a bone that is broken. There might be certain muscles you want to strengthen.

Once you've decided on the physical, emotional, or mental area you want to make strong, say aloud three times, "I call strength to my mind (heart, legs, etc.)." Then inhale sharply, sucking the ball of light into whatever area you have named. Picture the ball of light inside you, and feel it spreading a warm glow. Feel that area relax and absorb strength.

If there's more than one area you want to strengthen, no problem. Look in your strongbox. Another ball of light awaits your call. And as soon as you use that one, another ball of dazzling light will pop up. Your power can be shut away and buried, but it can't be depleted. However often you need strength, and for however long, your power is there for you.

50

CALMING THE WATERS

What do you do when you get riled up? How do you handle those stormy days that assault your otherwise sunny nature? Here's an image to use to restore calm.

Most chemical activity in your body requires water, and therefore over half your body is composed of water. It could be said that you are a body of water. What body of water do you most resemble? A large lake? A deep lagoon? A wide river? An ocean?

Take a moment to get a clear sense of yourself as a particular body of water. How large are you? How deep are you? Is your coastline smoothly curved or irregular? Is it edged with sand, rocky cliffs, or lush foliage?

A storm has blown in and whipped your waters into angry whitecaps. Rain lashes against you. The color of the water has turned from clear blue to menacing black. A storm surge has caused giant swells, and furious waves crash along your coastline, eroding it. Where once fish and dolphin frolicked, piranha and sharks now lurk. You're flooded with turmoil. Thunder booms and lightning flashes. Family and friends who were out boating have become dreadfully seasick, and their boats are about to capsize.

You feel helpless to stem the tide of emotion. The more helpless you feel, the more the storm intensifies. Before you drown in the storm, ask for help. Go ahead, yell for help into the very storm itself.

As soon as you ask for help, help appears. A treasure chest dredged up by the storm from a sunken galleon washes to shore at your feet. Opening it you find an inscription inside the lid: "Herein lie the Seeds of Calm." The chest is brimming with sunny golden seeds. What size are they? What shape?

Grab two fistfuls of the Seeds of Calm and face the stormy waters. Rain beats on your face. Wind whips your hair. Yet standing there you suddenly seem to draw strength from the elements. You pull solidity from the ground on which you stand. The wind clears

MENTAL AND EMOTIONAL HEALTH

your thoughts. The rain cleanses you. A lightning bolt brings illumination.

You feel charged with power, and in charge. Lifting your arms above your head, fists closed around the Seeds of Calm, you shout into the storm, commanding it to be calm. Then you hurl your seeds across the water. A gust of wind comes from behind, helping to scatter the seeds far and wide.

The storm abates. The winds die down. The driving rain turns to drizzle. The waves diminish. Family and friends sail safely to shore, smiling broadly.

Grab more fistfuls of Seeds of Calm and fling them over the water. The seeds sink deep into the water, turning it from black to blue. Waves disappear, leaving a calm surface. The rain ceases altogether, and the biting wind becomes a gentle breeze.

Once more you toss the Seeds of Calm high and wide across the water. The sun appears. It burns away the remaining clouds and dries your soggy clothes. It warms your soul. It brightens your day.

When angry storms strike, picture your emotional waters becoming dark and choppy. Then picture your treasure chest containing a lifetime supply of Seeds of Calm, so you'll never run out. Fling fistfuls of seeds across the waters to restore calm and bring out the sun.

123
▼

51

CHILD'S PLAY

It's today. Do you know where your inner child is? No matter what age you are—twenty-one or ninety-one—or how adult, you have a child self who lives in the timeless world of your thoughts and feelings.

Depending on whether your child self is sad or glad, he (or she) can either be inhibiting or enhancing your life as an adult. Either way it is in your best interests to befriend your child self. If he's sad, and leaking his sadness into your adult life, you can stop the leak by comforting him and making him feel better. If he's happy, you can bring his valuable curiosity and spontaneity into your adult life by playing with him.

Form a picture in your mind of yourself as a child at an age when you were fairly well co-ordinated physically and verbally, somewhere between five and seven years old. What do you look like? How is your hair cut? What are you wearing? What do you smell of? Are you chubby or thin? What are you doing? Are you running around carefree, or are you being careful not to get dirty? What's the expression on your face? Smiling? Curious? Angry? Crying?

Once you have a vivid picture or sense of your child self, talk to him. Introduce yourself as a friend. You might begin by saying, "Hi. My name is _____. What's yours?" His name might be a secret name, a nickname, or the same as yours is now. Then say, "I'd like to be your friend." Ask him, "What would you like to do today?"

With an open heart and an open mind, listen to what your child self says. Then take his hand and play with him. Maybe you play soldiers, or house, or hide-and-seek. Or go swimming, or to the circus. Do whatever your child wants to do regardless of whether or not you actually did that as a child. Just have fun. Find out what he thinks and feels about his world. Get his imagination going.

After you've spent some time with your child self, ask him what he wants. Whatever he wants, give it to him. It could be anything from a hug to a pony. Wrap it up or make it special in some way. Be sure to give him what he wants with no strings attached. He doesn't have to tidy up his toys, or be good, or eat all his brussels sprouts in order to get what he wants. He can have it just because you love him.

Don't worry about spoiling him; that's not a concern here. The idea is to play with your inner child and give him what he wants so that you get to know your child self and to appreciate him—and he you.

Doing this also allows you to heal any hurts he has. If he's sad, put your arms around him and comfort him. Let him know you're there and ask him what he needs. Kiss his scrapes and bruises whether they be physical or emotional. Put large Band-Aids on the boo-boos on his knee, or his elbow, or his heart.

If he's angry, give him permission to release his anger in the safety of your mind. Let him kick and scream and throw things. You're an adult—you can take it. And make sure he knows that you still love him even when he's angry.

Your child self is part of who you are. By getting to know your child self, you get to know your adult self. Whatever you do for your child self in terms of giving love, comfort, and forgiveness, you do the same for yourself. In short, encouraging an exchange of love between adult and child benefits both. Whenever you need a boost in spirit, take a couple of minutes to summon up your child self, and play away.

52

TAKING A BREATHER

Have you had so much to do that you've been racing about pell-mell, never stopping for a second? Stop and smell the roses? Are you kidding—there's barely been time to wake up and smell the coffee. You need to take a breather, literally and figuratively.

Find a comfortable chair. Sit in it with your back straight and your legs uncrossed, feet flat on the floor. Focus your attention on your breathing, letting all other thoughts and concerns drift away. If a worry intrudes, don't worry it to death, just return your attention to your breathing. Feel the rhythm of your breath. Feel grateful for how you go on breathing whether you're paying attention or not. Be thankful for each life-giving breath.

As you begin to relax, picture, or sense, a bubble of light floating in front of the upper part of your face, covering your nose. The light might be bright white, a rainbow of colors, or a single color: splendor lavender, cool blue, serene green, mellow yellow, exchange orange, or wink pink.

In front of the lower part of your face, covering your mouth, is another bubble of light that is bright white. Focus first on the upper bubble of light, inhaling the light through your nose. Make it a long, slow breath. If you want to count as you inhale, use your heartbeat as a metronome. Breathe in the light, smoothly and deeply. Let the fresh oxygen spread out from your lungs, bringing bright energy into every part of your body. If there is an area that is especially tense, direct the light to that area.

Exhale through your mouth into the lower bubble of bright white light. Again, if you want to count to keep your breathing even, use your heartbeat as a guide. As you exhale, breathe out tension, frustration, and pain. Depending on how stressed you are, it might look like gray smoke coming out of your mouth, or brown smog, or even black soot. Your subconscious will show you how severe your stress level is by how dark the air is coming out of your mouth.

When you exhale dark tension into the lower bubble of white light, a wondrous thing happens. As soon as the dark hits the light, it's transformed into light. Pain is instantly healed and transmuted. The white light is composed of thousands of tiny tension-absorbing sparkles that gobble up darkness and convert it to light.

Continue to breathe deeply and evenly until the air coming out of your mouth is clear. If pressed for time, breathing can be done for a minute or two at intervals throughout the day to restore energy and concentration. The upper bubble of light constantly replenishes itself, so there is always an abundance of healthy, refreshing light to breathe.

With every inhale-exhale breathing cycle you feel more relaxed, more open. You're not only breathing fresh air into yourself, but into your life. Be thankful for each life-giving breath. When life is so rushed that you feel short of breath, take a breather.

53

MELTING FEAR

Have you ever been so afraid that you felt frozen by fear? Couldn't move? Could barely breathe? Whenever fear threatens to stop you cold, use the following visualization to overcome it.

Sometimes just thinking about something you're afraid of doing can bring on fear. Maybe you're afraid to ask for a raise, or fly in a plane, or go to the dentist. When it comes to doing it, you can't. An ice cube forms in the pit of your stomach. Icicles of fear spread through you. Soon you feel numb, frozen in a block of ice.

Picture the block of ice. How thick is it? How big? Is your head free? Can you move your arms and legs, or are you completely encased in ice? Unable to move? Unable to take action?

When you look out through the thick ice of fear it blurs your view of reality. In the same way, the fear frozen around you distorts people's view of you.

The size of the block of ice is the size of your fear. The block of ice weighs you down and limits what you can do. You can't go places you want to go. Or touch people. Or get what you need. The block of ice blocks you!

Do you want to stay frozen in fear? The obvious answer is *no*. But sometimes people *like* to be immobilized by fear because it gives them an excuse not to do something that they secretly don't want to do anyway. But more often than not, fear keeps you from doing something positive. It's up to you. You can stay frozen in fear, or free yourself from it.

Get rid of the cold, thick, heavy fear-ice surrounding you, but don't make the process difficult. Let your imagination have fun with it.

Here are some ways you can eliminate the chill of fear:

Want to break the ice? Call in a specially trained squad to help you. "Fearbusters" is emblazoned on their uniforms. Using huge mallets they hammer the ice into smithereens. Or they spray the block of ice with hot water. Or drill holes in it. Or make a tunnel for you to crawl out through.

Or imagine that you are outdoors and the warm noonday sun melts the block of ice—effortlessly.

Or maybe your body starts generating so much heat that it melts the ice from the inside.

Picture an operatic soprano standing nearby. When she sings, the high notes shatter the ice.

Have a wise old magician stand in front of you. He waves his magic wand and the block of ice swings open, freeing you.

Think of your own ways to dissolve fear.

Don't let fear freeze you out of life. Whenever you feel the chill of fear creeping into your bones, take charge! Melt it! Bust it!

54

WALL FALL

Have you built a wall around yourself? If you have, you probably did it for protection, the same way that early cities were surrounded with a wall in order to keep out marauders and enemies. The problem with a wall is that it doesn't discriminate between friends and foes; at the same time that you're keeping out foes, you're also keeping out friends.

The second problem is that not only does a wall keep people out, it keeps you in. Your thoughts, feelings, and activities are held back and limited by the wall.

The third problem with building a wall around yourself is that it blocks your view of the outside world, and blocks the outside world's view of you.

These might be the results you wanted when you originally built the wall. You might have erected a wall during a crisis, or at a time of extreme vulnerability, when you needed to regroup and heal. The wall might have been useful as a temporary measure, but if left in place permanently, a wall prevents you from living fully.

Imagine that you're standing in front of your wall. Take a good look at it. What material is it made of? Wood? Brick? Concrete? How high is it? How thick?

A few feet to your right you see a sturdy ladder leaning against the wall. Curious, you walk over and climb up the ladder until you can see over the top of the wall. What you see is a lush green meadow carpeted with bright flowers. In the meadow are friends who wave and invite you over. Also in the meadow is that job or promotion you've been wanting. A new home or car. A grove of money trees. A loving partner. Whatever you've been desiring is there.

What you see looks so inviting that you have a strong urge to be on the other side of the wall. There are any number of ways that you can accomplish this. Your enthusiasm gives you the strength to leap easily over the wall, dropping gently onto soft ground. Or you climb back down the ladder and find a way through the wall. Maybe you see a door that you hadn't noticed before and you go through it. Call in your Blockbusters to unleash their power to smash the wall to smithereens.

Without the protection of the wall you could feel vulnerable. Replace the wall with a non-limiting form of protection such as a bubble of bright white light. The light surrounds you completely, reaching from head to toe, and from one outstretched fingertip to the other.

Light keeps out darkness. It lets in friends but keeps out foes. It allows for an exchange of thoughts and feelings between you and others. It moves with you. And not only does it allow you to see the world, and the world to see you, but it illuminates both. The light is a more flexible and more powerful form of protection than the wall. It enables you to give and receive happiness, to grow.

As soon as the wall falls, you run eagerly into the meadow. Friends and family throw their arms around you—they couldn't before because the wall separated you from them. You in turn embrace them as well as the goal you wanted. You feel free, glad all over. Happiness spills out of you, causing flowers to spring up around your feet. Maybe you do a cartwheel or a handstand.

If, during a crisis, you begin building a wall around yourself out of habit—stop. Destroy whatever wall you've put up, and put light around you instead. The bubble of light is as real as the wall, but much more effective and life-enhancing.

55
HEARTFELT

Has your heart been taking a beating? Has it been bruised by disappointment? Does it ache with loss? Is it tense with anger? Has pain closed its doors? If your heart could use some tender loving care, this visualization's for you.

First form a picture of your heart in your mind—or a sense of it. You might imagine an anatomical heart, or something symbolic like a Valentine heart, or a heart-shaped light that gently pulsates.

What kind of shape is your heart in? Does it glow with health, beating with a strong, steady rhythm? Or does it seem defeated, its appearance dim and gray with a faint or irregular heartbeat?

Get to the heart of the matter. Ask your heart how it feels. Keeping an open mind, listen to its response. If your heart is feeling kinda low, don't reprimand it for feeling that way. Instead, acknowledge that it hurts, and offer comfort and understanding. Ask your heart, "What can I do to help? Is there something I can do to make you feel better?"

With a kind mind, listen to its answer. Then do whatever your heart needs or wants—TLC is definitely in order.

• Maybe your heart needs to be hugged, or cradled, or rocked. If it does, put your arms around it.

• Is there a soothing song you could sing to it?

• Would it enjoy a gentle massage?

• Maybe it wants to be bathed and have the grime of pain rinsed away by clear water. Or you could give it a bubble bath.

• Soak out heartache in warm water to which Epsom salts have been added.

• If your heart is broken, call in a "heart fixer" to repair it—he or she has whatever tools are necessary to do the job.

• If it's torn, mend it.

• If it has a hole, patch it up.

• If it's closed down, pull off the boards and unlock the door.

- If it's empty and abandoned, fill it with love light.
- Present it with a bouquet of flowers, or a single rose.
- Tell it, "I love you."

Give your heart whatever it wants and needs—and lots of it. Give it what it needs to be whole, and healthy, and strong. After all, your heart beats day after day for you. Offer your sincere thanks for its efforts.

Picture your heart glowing with health. Hear it beating with a strong, steady beat. Feel it being happy inside you. Feel it feeling loved and loving.

It's helpful to give your heart loving attention on a regular basis. Give it plenty of TLC in return for all it does for you. Then, instead of your heart taking a beating, you'll help it to go on beating.

56

PUTTING OUT ANGER

If you're human and interacting with the world, chances are good that someone or something is going to make you angry sometime. Maybe you do a slow burn when you're angry, or explode on a short fuse. Whether you're hot tempered, or just plain angry, this visualization can help you release anger safely and then douse the angry flames.

In what place or places do you tend to become angry? At home? At work? In a car? Where you play sports? Where you socialize? Picture the place where you are most often angry. See or sense it clearly enough so that you can recall a particular detail about the surroundings.

Once you can see the place, picture a fire burning there, paying particular attention to just where the fire is burning. For example, if you get angry in a car, does the fire burn in the driver's seat or the passenger seat? If you become angry at home, where in the house does the fire burn? In the living room because living makes you angry? In the bedroom because you're angry with your partner? With your children in their room? In the kitchen around issues of giving or receiving nourishment? Does the fire start in one room and spread to another?

Take a good look at each fire, noticing details. What fuels the fire? How big is it? How high do the flames leap? What color are they? How hot is it? Is the fire contained, or does it rage out of control? How do you feel about the fire: are you afraid of it or proud of it? Is the fire hurting anyone? Is it destroying property?

Allow the images of the fire to come to mind without censoring them, because these mental pictures contain valuable insights as to when, where, and why you get angry. Anger itself is without form, but by seeing anger as fire, you can more easily see how your anger burns and the impact it has.

Once you have located and defined your anger, you can use the mental image of a fire burning as a way to safely release your anger without actually harming others, yourself, or property. In your mind, let the fire burn for a couple of minutes at home, in your office, in your car, on the tennis court, at a club, etc. Focus on the fire burning. See the flames leap. Hear them crackle. Feel the heat. Smell the smoke. Then put out the fire.

How you extinguish the fire will depend on its size and what's fueling it. If the fire is small and contained, douse it with a bucket of water. Hear the flames sputter and hiss. If the fire is fueled by oil or grease, throw sand on it. Smother it with a blanket. Grab a fire extinguisher to spew foam on the flames.

If your anger is a three-alarm fire raging out of control, call the fire department to help put it out. Picture a fire engine clanging to a stop in front of your house. Firefighters pour off the truck, uncoiling hoses and drenching everything with hundreds of gallons of water. Smell the acrid smoke hanging in the air.

After the fire is extinguished, check to see what damage has been done. If your anger has burned someone, put salve on his or her injuries. If property has been damaged, picture it being repaired. Do whatever you need to in order to make everyone and everything whole again. Apologize sincerely for any harm you've done.

After the fire has been extinguished, light a candle where once your anger burned. The candle can be white or some soft color. The flickering flame casts a gentle light; its glow is a reminder of peace.

57

MOON-ENLIGHTEN

Have you been carrying around unnecessary baggage from the past? Old emotions and memories that you've packed away, but no longer need? Old patterns of behavior that aren't bringing desirable results? Crammed into your mental and emotional luggage might be limiting beliefs, negative attitudes, painful memories, worries, unloving relationships, failed endeavors, resentments. Here's a way to pack up your cares and woes and ship them out so you no longer have to spend your energy lugging them around.

Imagine that you're standing on a sandy shore at night, facing a pond, a lake, or the sea. The sand is warm beneath your feet. A soft breeze curls freely about your body. High in the sky, directly in front of you, shines a full moon. It cuts a swath of moonlight across the water, like a river of light that flows right to you.

Pulled up on shore is a rowboat with the bow pointing toward you. Painted on one side of the bow is your name, and on the other side, "Full Moon." It's a beamy rowboat with a couple of wide wooden seats and a squared-off stern.

All the baggage you want to get rid of is piled on the shore around you, ready to load into the rowboat. Each piece is identified according to its contents. A briefcase with a broken handle and the initials "L.B." contains limiting beliefs. Open it and check to see that you've packed every outmoded belief. Beliefs might be written on pieces of paper, or take a symbolic form such as broken mirrors. Toss the briefcase into the rowboat.

A shabby old leather suitcase has the initials "P.M." for painful memories. It's full of old pictures, cracked and faded. Are there any you forgot to pack? Lug the suitcase to the boat and load it in. A stained duffel bag is so heavy that it feels as if lead weights are in it. The word *Anger* is stenciled on its side. A nylon knapsack is bulky with *Problems*. If there are people with whom you've had unsatisfying relationships—romantic, personal, or business—help them to seats in your *Full Moon* rowboat. If you need help loading, ask and help will appear.

The boat is sturdy and can hold loads of baggage as well as several people. If you have more to ship than fits on the boat, it can make another trip. Once the boat is full, swing the bow around so it's pointing out to sea. Hear it scrape against the sand. Line up the bow with the bright, wide river of moonlight shimmering on the sea, and shove the rowboat into the water.

Standing on the shore you notice that the stern is painted with the words, *Bye-Bye*. At first the boat just bobs in the water, but then the magnetic force of the moon grabs hold of the bow and pulls the boat forward.

The pull of the moon is so powerful that it lifts the bow of the rowboat right out of the water, and the entire rowboat glides up the river of moonlight through the starry night sky. You watch as the rowboat, laden with all your cares and woes, gets smaller and smaller. It's a mere speck as it nears the moon, and then it disappears completely.

As soon as the boat disappears from sight, the weight of your past disappears too. Released from carrying that excess baggage around, a new sense of freedom, like a breeze, curls up from your toes and spirals around your body. You give thanks to the full moon for taking your old emotional and mental baggage. Flooded with energy as bright and strong as the moonlight, you're ready for the future.

Use this visualization to unload yourself of old baggage whenever you feel the need. It's especially powerful to do on an actual night of a full moon. If you feel that you have several loads to get rid of, do the visualization three nights in a row; the night before the full moon, the night of, and the night after. Be moon-enlightened.

58

BREAK OUT

Are you sometimes a prisoner of negative thinking? Do dark thoughts ever prevent you from enjoying life? This visualization can be the key to freedom!

Imagine yourself in a narrow prison cell, surrounded by impenetrable steel bars. An oily sweat oozes from the gray floor and walls. Rats scratch in the corners and cockroaches rustle brazenly across the filthy floor. The air is sour and stale with the smell of frustration and failure. A faucet drips relentlessly, and the toilet is stopped up. A bare bulb sheds a murky, yellow light.

These are how your negative thoughts might look if they had form. They trap you in despair and separate you from life.

And there you sit, huddled in a corner, head buried between your updrawn knees. Someone stops at the door to your cell and calls your name. You don't look up or answer. Again they say your name and ask if you need anything. You mumble, "No," keeping your head down.

A third time, the person says your name and asks if they can help you. Their persistence and tone of concern finally get your attention. Tiredly, you raise your head.

The person standing outside your prison cell could be either a man or a woman. It might be someone you love, or who loves you. It might be a kindly stranger who stands outside your cell in the Prison of Negative Thoughts. Someone aglow with the strength that comes from within.

You ask, "Please, let me out." Without hesitation this new-found ally agrees. In fact, he or she has been waiting for you to *ask*. From a ring of keys the person selects an old brass key and unlocks the door to your cell. Hear it turn in the lock.

Your liberator swings your cell door wide open. Hear it open. As you walk through the wide open door you feel as if a hundred tons of weight have been lifted from you. Once beyond the door you look back at your cramped, dank, dark cell. You say good-bye to it, slamming the door shut with finality. Hear the resounding clang of it shutting.

Gratefully, you shake your liberator's hand. With a wide grin he or she leads the way out of the Prison of Negative Thoughts.

Eager to be free, you race pell-mell down the gray cement corridors. Gates open magically before you. Anyone who challenges you or tries to stop you is quickly dispatched by your liberator. Finally the last thick, heavy, metal door swings opens to the outside.

You burst through into bright sunlight. You're in a lush, green spring meadow carpeted with flowers. Clear blue sky arches overhead. A sparkling stream meanders under stately trees. Breathless from running, you fall onto the soft grass, stretching out on your back, laughing delightedly. Taking deep gulps of the fresh, sweet air, you feel so light you could almost float. The meadow represents how positive thoughts might look if they took form.

Gently the sun warms your skin. Birds swoop and glide above your head, chirping and cheering your release. After you've caught your breath, you rise to your feet and start jumping for joy. You feel free. You *are* free! Glad to be alive. Expanded. Buoyant. You notice that you're thinking positive thoughts about yourself and your future. A powerful feeling that you can accomplish whatever you set your mind to grows within you.

Whenever you feel negative thoughts threatening to imprison you, focus on the sunny merriment of the Meadow of Positive Thoughts. Let the vibrant feeling of being free enliven you.

59

MAKE IT SHINE

Ever have one of those days when you feel as if you're walking around under a dark cloud? While the sun seems to be shining on everyone else, you feel like a storm waiting to happen. Here are some ways to change your forecast from cloudy to clear and sunny.

Take a few seconds to picture what that cloud over your head looks like. How big is it? Does the shadow around you extend just a couple of feet, or for yards? How thick is it? Is it a towering thunderhead, or a mild spring rain cloud? What color is the cloud? Just-okay off-white? Sad gray? Or angry black? Once you can define the cloud, it's easier to deal with.

You may or may not know what caused the cloud to form. It could be disappointment, frustration, fatigue, hurt, anger, negative thinking, illness, etc. Fortunately, you don't have to know how the cloud got there in order to make it disappear.

Before you get rid of the cloud you might see if it's serving any particular purpose. You can ask yourself or ask the cloud. Maybe it's bringing some necessary rain into your life and will actually help things grow. Or it's there to block out the sun because you don't want to "see the light" about something. Maybe you've been working hard and need an excuse to rest and receive some caring attention.

Decide how you want to get rid of the cloud. Be silly or sublime about it. You could imagine that you put up a big, strong umbrella and let the cloud rain itself out. The rain pours down, complete with the excitement of thunder and lightning if you want to go for drama.

Or you let it rain itself out and don't mind getting wet. Maybe you get naked and let the rain pour down your body, cleansing it. Then the sun comes out and dries you, and you put on dry, brand-new clothes.

You could simply step out from under the cloud, letting it rain on a patch of land where you've planted the seeds of success. Watch them sprout.

Knowing that the sun is shining somewhere above you, you direct the sun's energy to dissipate the cloud.

Plant your feet sturdily upon the earth, cup your hands around your mouth, look up at the cloud, and shout, *"Go away!"* Shout it with unmistakable authority and intent. Shout *"Go away"* three times, or until the cloud goes away.

Imagine that there's a "cloud collector" who patrols the sky. You summon him or her to come and collect your cloud. He or she stuffs it in a giant garbage sack and hauls it away.

The cloud is blown away by a blast of wind.

Sprinkle your cloud with Disappearing Dust, and watch it vanish into thin air.

Turn your cloud pink. Or give it polka dots. How about stripes? Take the seriousness out of your cloud and you take away its power over you.

Whenever you feel as if it's raining on your parade of life, take a couple of minutes to make that dark cloud disappear. Then revel in the sunshine.

60

PEACE PAINT

Are you at war with yourself or others? Or are there just a few too many trouble spots in the world to suit you? Well, instead of putting on the war paint, use this visualization to grab your can of peace paint and start painting your world peaceful.

What would peace look like in liquid form? Soothingly blue-green like the sea? White like milk? Clear and golden like honey? Pink like watermelon juice? Thick? Creamy?

Whatever peace in liquid form looks like to you, picture a big paint can of it. The can is clearly marked on the side: "Peace Paint." Prying off the lid, you see that it's only about half full of peace—as opposed to being half empty. It looks so delicious that you dip your finger in; it tastes sweet and smooth. What does it smell like?

Alongside the can of peace is a large, wide paintbrush. What color are the bristles? Golden? Black? Purple? White? The brush is light when you pick it up, and it fits in your hand as if it were made for you.

Peace begins within, so dip the brush in the peace paint and paint whatever areas of yourself are in conflict: mind, heart, stomach, etc. The paint soaks into those areas, calming them. Then picture anyone with whom you're at war, and slap a generous coat of peace paint on them.

Once you and the people in your immediate world are coated with peace, turn your attention to the world in general. Imagine that you're sitting or standing on a white, puffy cloud, floating high above the earth. You might see the earth as a globe, or a map, or a topographical model. It doesn't have to be pictured in perfect detail, just a sense of it will do fine.

Like a zoom lens on a camera, you can focus on whatever area of the world you choose, as close or as far away as you want. Wherever you focus, your cloud whisks you there at the speed of thought.

You might choose to focus first on the place where you live, on the theory that peace begins at home. Picture the house or building in which you live as seen from above. Then dipping the paintbrush into the peace bucket, paint your home with peace. The peace paint glides on smoothly.

Pulling back your focus just a bit, you see the city where you live spread out below you. Paint your town or city with peace paint, and feel a sense of calm spread over it. Ooops—better check the level of paint in the can. Surprise! Surprise! The can is now full to the brim with peace paint because the more peace you spread, the more peace there is.

Continue to shift your focus at the speed of thought, spreading peace paint across the state in which you live, adjacent states, across the country and adjacent countries, until you have painted the entire planet. Cities, states, countries, islands, continents (don't forget Antarctica), hemispheres, and oceans are coated with sweet peace. Some areas may not take the paint well and will require a primer coat. Other areas soak up the peace paint so quickly that they require a second coat.

This is a helpful visualization to do once a week, or at least once a month. When there's news of a particular area of the world that's at war, or which has experienced some kind of disaster—flooding, earthquake, fire, tornado, hurricane—grab your brush and your peace paint, and slather it on. Tilt the bucket and let peace pour out.

No matter how weathered and worn the world might look to you, there's always enough peace paint in your can to paint the world with peace. Apply as often as necessary.

PHYSICAL HEALTH

61

WILLING WELLNESS

When you're not feeling up to snuff, or are downright sick, a positive mental attitude is a real ally in getting well. But often when your body is feeling weak and disabled, or is in pain, your will to be healthy can be similarly affected. Here's a way to strengthen and heal your will to be well so it can help you become healthier.

Imagine that your will to be well has form. It might assume human form, male or female, real or fictitious: a doctor, a fairy godmother, a grandparent, an Indian chief, Wonder Woman, or a sage. It might be an animal such as a lion or a bear, or even Mighty Mouse. It could come to mind as a creature such as a leprechaun or Yoda.

Take a moment to see, or sense, your will to be well. Is it large or small? Rosy bright, or dim gray? Does it stand tall, or is it slumped over in a corner? Is it hot or cold? What kind of sound does it make?

Your subconscious will let you know what kind of shape your will to be healthy is in by the pictures that come into your mind. If your will looks puny and defeated, and is a gray-green-brown color, it's in no condition to help improve *your* condition. If you help your will to be healthy, it can help you to be healthy.

Begin by saying hello to whatever form your will has assumed, and introducing yourself. "Hello. My name is _____." You may sense-hear your will saying hello in return, perhaps in a tired, thin voice. Ask it its name and see if a name pops into your mind. Use that name whenever you talk with your will.

Ask your will, "How are you?" Listen kindly to what it says. Then ask it, "What do you need to feel better?" Maybe your will is hungry. Ask what it likes to eat and picture a huge platter of its favorite food. If your will is too weak to feed itself, spoon-feed it. With every bite your will becomes bigger, and stronger, and brighter, until it's able to feed itself. Keep an ample supply of its favorite foods in mind so it doesn't go hungry.

Or maybe your will needs attention and a friendly hug. Tell your will that you want to be friends and put your arms around it. What does it feel like to hug your will? Is it soft? Bony? Prickly? Smooth? As you hug it, your will perks up, grows bigger, and turns a rosy color. Tell your will something that you like about it. As you hug and praise your will, its negative energy is transmuted into positive. Your will to be well looks more and more healthy and attractive.

Ask your will what kind of environment it feels strongest in. A picture might come to mind of a turquoise tropical beach, or a meadow abloom with spring flowers, or a magical room somewhere in time and space. Picture your will in that place of strength. Feel it being big and powerful. It's full of energy and ready for action.

Reassure your will that you want to be friends and that you'll help it to stay strong. Ask your will to help you become strong and healthy, too. It readily agrees. The two of you shake on it. Or you sense-hear it say, "Yes." Or it gives you a hug. Or all of the above.

Picture yourself standing together with your will in its place of power. You enjoy a deep feeling of peace and satisfaction knowing that you have helped your will to be well to be well. It fills you with comfort to know that you now have an ally in health. You see yourself becoming more and more healthy, more vibrant.

62

FOUNTAIN OF HEALTH

Almost five hundred years ago Ponce de Leon searched for the fountain of youth. He may have been looking in all the wrong places. It's possible that the true fountain of youth and its counterpart, the fountain of health, aren't to be found in Florida or any other physical locale, but that they exist within. Health and youth begin as concepts that flow deep within our subconscious. There's no time like the present to discover your inner fountain of health.

Imagine that you're walking on a path where rocky cliffs rise against a bright blue sky. Hear the sound of your footsteps. Is the path made of dirt or crushed rock? Look down to see what kind of footgear you're wearing. Look at your hands.

The crisp, clear day is invigorating. Rounding a bend to your right, you find yourself at the opening of a cave. Curious, you take a few hesitant steps inside and find an old miner's lantern. You dig some matches out of your jacket pocket and, wonder of wonders, the lantern catches, casting a wide circle of golden light into the darkness of the cave. You feel safe.

Drawn irresistibly deeper into the cave, making your way is easy with the aid of the lantern. You reach the back of the cave where the vaulted ceiling and the floor meet. Raising the lantern high, you discover a tunnel just a little taller and wider than you are. You enter. The light of the lantern reflects off the rough-hewn sides of the tunnel, revealing a thick vein of gold.

At the end of the tunnel are steps cut into the rock leading down. Count each step as you descend. The last step is inlaid with the numbers of your birthdate spelled out in turquoise.

Ahead stretches a hall, at the end of which is a flickering glow. As you hurry down the hall you hear a musical splashing sound that gets louder and louder, stirring greater and greater excitement within you.

Bursting through the end of the hallway you find yourself in a high-ceilinged oval chamber. In the center is your very own fountain of health. It shines and splashes, the water cascading down over seven golden tiers, each round tier increasing in diameter from the spire at the top to a large pool at the bottom.

The water glows with a powerful inner luminescence that lights the entire chamber. The floor, walls, and domed ceiling of the chamber are made of amethyst, rose quartz, and crystal-clear quartz. Thick veins of gold and silver run through them. The chamber hums with energy.

In the fountain, subtle colors shift and slide through the streams of water: raspberry pinks, mint greens, champagne golds. As you near the fountain the spray from the splashing water mists your face and arms. On an amethyst ledge near the fountain is a champagne glass. You pluck it off the ledge and use it to catch the water as it splashes merrily from one tier to another.

Bringing the brimming glass to your lips, you sip this liquid of life and health. As it glides across your tongue its effervescence titillates your taste buds with a flavor at once sweet, tart, and mysterious. With each swallow this elixir of youth cascades down your throat and flows through your body where it is absorbed.

The water from the fountain of health cleanses every cell in your body, reminding it of its right to be healthy. It melts away discord and disease. It revitalizes every part of you so that you feel your body come alive. It feels like thousands of lights blinking on within you and twinkling like stars.

You climb into the large golden pool at the bottom of the fountain. Youth juice sluices over your body from the tiers above, rinsing away tension lines and firming skin.

Once you've discovered your fountain of health, you can visit it anytime you want to. Just picture the quartz chamber with the fountain of health shining and splashing in the center. Then treat yourself to a drink of youth juice and a bath in the health-restoring waters.

63
DOCTOR META

Once upon a time doctors-who-made-house-calls roamed the land in large numbers, tending to their patients. But the number of people increased rapidly, making it more difficult for doctors to visit everyone who was sick. At the same time, the number of cars increased, making it easier for people to visit the doctor. In just a few years, doctors-who-made-house-calls became almost extinct.

But take heart. You can have a doctor-who-makes-house-calls. Your own personal physician who's on call 24 hours a day, 7 days a week, 52 weeks a year. A doctor who never plays golf, or is at a fundraiser, or is away on vacation. A doctor who is wise and caring, with a thorough knowledge of all fields of medicine.

A doctor like that sounds out of this world, doesn't he? Well, he is. You could call him a *metaphysician* because he isn't physical. Dr. Meta. He's alive and well and practicing medicine in your mind. All you have to do is call his name the instant you feel unwell, and he arrives immediately.

This is your dream doctor come true, so make it good. What does he look like? Is he a kindly country doctor arriving with his little black bag full of instruments and medicine? Or is he a young space-age doctor who arrives jet propelled, with a metallic black case full of computer probes and healants? What is he wearing? A frock coat? A white lab jacket? A metallic mesh jumpsuit? What nationality is he? Is he gray-haired or not? Does he wear glasses? What color are his eyes?

Get a feel for Dr. Meta. His caring. His wisdom. Just having him there makes you feel better. He sits across from you, or if you're sick in bed he pulls up a chair beside you. His manner is gentle and unhurried. He asks you how you feel. You tell him every ache and pain you have, both the physical and the non-physical ones.

Dr. Meta listens carefully, nodding his head attentively. He asks more questions, probing for details. He makes it clear that your well-being is his utmost concern.

After you've told him how you feel, Dr. Meta examines you. He might listen to your heart, shine a light into your eyes and ears, press here and there, flex an arm or a knee, take your temperature, or do a blood pressure reading. Perhaps he takes a moment to ponder his findings, or he feeds data into a computer. As soon as Dr. Meta is sure of his diagnosis, he tells you what it is. He tells you clearly and honestly in terms that you can understand. His eyes shine with compassion as he speaks his mind to your mind.

After telling you the diagnosis, Dr. Meta might suggest what measures to take to help your body regain its healthy balance. Or tell you how long the healing process will take. If necessary, he might bring in a colleague to assist.

Dr. Meta might prescribe rest or exercise. He might tell you to eat or avoid certain foods. He might give you a special healing elixir to swallow, or a painless injection. He might give you a space-age healant, or rub a magical healing salve into the areas that hurt. He could lay his hand gently upon you, healing you with his touch, gentle warmth radiating from his hand into your body. Or if something needs to come out, he reaches into your body and pulls it out—no mess, no fuss, no pain.

Whether your ailment is minor or major, you trust Dr. Meta to help you get well—painlessly! Whatever you need in the way of medical attention, Dr. Meta provides it, and at no charge. Dr. Meta is indeed out of this world, but when you call, he comes. His one desire is to make you well.

64

POOL COOL

Has Murphy's Law been running amok? Or does just everyday life make you tense? Are you clouded with mental worry? Has the emotional climate been stormy? Are you physically uptight? Use this mental image to relax.

Imagine that you're floating on your back on a raft in a swimming pool. The pool filter gurgles softly. You trail one hand in the cool, clear turquoise water. A gentle breeze plays across your body. Overhead, the sky is a sea of blue.

The sun feels soothingly warm upon your body. It massages the soles of your feet and tickles the tops of your toes. Cozily slippered in sun, your feet relax and your toes uncurl.

Feel the sun on your ankles and legs, on your knees and thighs. Release all tension to the sun.

Feel the warm glow of the sun on your pelvis and hips, and on your stomach. The sun's warmth penetrates your skin and is soaked up by your body. Wherever the sun touches, it absorbs all pain and tension and carries it away.

Beams of sunlight dance on your chest, reaching gently into your heart to lift out all physical and emotional pain. Feeling soothed by the sun, you breathe more calmly, more fully.

Become aware of the sun massaging your shoulders, arms, and hands. Feel them relax.

The sun's warmth moves up your neck to your throat. Any tightness in your throat melts away.

Feel the sun resting gently on your face, drawing tension from your temples and eyes. Worry empties from your mind. The sun warms the spot where your jaw hinges, and your jaw relaxes, dropping slightly.

Breathing in through your nose, you inhale the bright energy of the sun. Feel the warmth and light of the sun fill your lungs and spread throughout your body. Direct extra light and warmth to any area that is especially tense or painful. Then breathe out through your mouth, exhaling stress like a dark cloud that immediately evaporates. Tension and doubt disappear in the light of the sun.

Turn over on your stomach. Feel the warmth of the sun on the back of your head, your neck, and your shoulders. Release tightness in these areas, allowing the sun to lift it away.

Slowly the sun's warmth moves down your back. Let it rest there, like a heating pad, until all aches are gone.

Feel the sun on your buttocks and the backs of your thighs. The backs of your knees and your calves receive the warmth of the sun and any muscle strain disappears.

Feel the sun again on the soles of your feet. Let the sun massage your feet and tickle your heels. You are now completely relaxed from head to toe.

Float on the raft in the clear turquoise water of the pool for as long as you want, whenever you want to relax. No matter how cloudy it may be in your physical landscape, in your mindscape it is always soothingly sunny.

65
PAIN-DESTROYER

Somewhere in your body, pain has you in its grip and is squeezing hard. Pain interferes with your ability to get things done. It wears you out and makes you cranky. Relief is just a visualization away.

Picture the door to your medicine cabinet. Opening it, you scan the familiar tubes and bottles on the shelves: toothpaste, shaving cream, aspirin, rubbing alcohol, Band-Aids, ointments, bottles of leftover prescriptions. Wait—what's this? A silver bottle with a label that reads: "Pain-Destroyer capsules. Effective within one hour. No harmful side-effects. Non-addicting." This is for you.

Uncapping the bottle you roll a sleek silver capsule into the palm of your hand. The pill is shaped like a tiny silver space capsule. This capsule seeks out pain, and then its tiny robot crew destroys the pain painlessly, without harming anything that's healthy.

Grab a glass of water or juice and pop the pain-destroyer capsule into your mouth. Swallow it down, launching it into your body. As soon as it hits your stomach its mission program is activated. Its sensors click on and it becomes fully activated. Using special radar it homes in on whatever territory has been taken over by pain. And as mission control, you can guide it too.

Swiftly, the pain-destroyer capsule zooms through your body, zeroing in on your pain. It might be that physical pain in your knee, your back, your shoulder, your stomach, or your head. Or it might be an emotional hurt such as the pain of loss.

Whatever the pain, and wherever it dwells, the pain-destroyer capsule lands right on target. The capsule hatch opens and the robot crew leaps out, armed and programmed to destroy pain. What do the crew members look like? How many of them are there? What color are they?

The pain-destroyer robots use their laser phasers to obliterate the coiled steel cable of pain that holds your back in a python-like grip. Or with blasters set at "Destroy," they shatter the black rock of pain in your head into microbits of dust. Or if the pain is caused by something broken or torn, they set their laser phasers to "Heal," and the bone, or muscle, or tissue, or emotion is repaired. If a deficiency—whether physical, mental, or emotional—is causing pain, the crew has whatever's needed in their well-stocked capsule.

The pain-destroyer crew reports "Mission accomplished," to you, mission control, and they and the capsule automatically deactivate and disintegrate. The grip of pain is loosened, its reign of tyranny is over. Pain no longer holds any power over you, or any part of you. Feel the pain release. The area, whether physical or non-physical, loosens. It's as if that area had been holding its breath in fear, and now it exhales and begins breathing freely.

Sighing deeply and satisfyingly, you do the same, directing fresh air to the area that was in pain. As you breathe oxygen into it, the area comes alive with energy and fills with life. Tell that area—whether it's your knee, your heart, or your mind—that it has full permission to be completely healthy and happy.

The remains of the capsule, and any debris from the destruction of the pain, are swept away by cleansing currents in your bloodstream and are eliminated naturally from your system. Within an hour of taking the pain-destroyer capsule, you are pain free.

The pain-destroyer capsules are harmful only to pain, not to you, so take one as needed. Don't let pain get a hold on you—destroy it with a pain-destroyer capsule.

66

TUNNEL CHARGE

When the future looks dark, rather than curse the darkness, turn on the lights. This visualization will light your way and give you energy.

Imagine that you are standing at the entrance to a tunnel. The tunnel stretches before you, a long tube of darkness. But glowing in the distance is the proverbial light at the end of the tunnel.

As your eyes adjust to the dim interior, you notice a light switch to your right. You flip the switch on, and a red bulb lights up over your head. Standing directly under the bulb, in the center of the circle of red light, bathe in the red glow. Let the strong, earthy red energy seep through your skin. Breathe in the red light and let it circulate throughout your body. It makes you feel strong and grounded.

When you've absorbed the red energy, take several steps forward. Be sure to leave the red light on behind you.

After a few steps you come to a second light switch and flip it on. A warm orange light shines. Bathe in the orange glow as you did in the red, allowing it to soak into you. Breathe in its powerful energy.

Leaving the orange light on, step forward again and flip on the third light switch. A sunny yellow light shines brightly above you. Draw its mentally stimulating energy into yourself.

With the yellow light still shining brightly, move on to the fourth light switch. You notice that the light at the end of the tunnel glows more brightly with every step you take toward it.

Flip on the fourth light switch and find yourself bathed in a clear, restful, green glow. The loving energy stimulates your heart, causing peaceful feelings to wash through your body like gentle waves.

Stepping forward again, you turn on the fifth light switch. A rich blue light shines overhead. As you stand within the circle of sparkling blue energy, you feel open and expressive.

Move on to the sixth light and flip it on. You're surrounded by a lavender glow, the color of lilacs in the spring. Soaking up the vibrant violet color, you feel more in touch with your intuitive self.

After you've absorbed the lavender light, take a few more steps forward. These steps bring you into the glowing white light at the end of the tunnel. This is one light you don't have to turn on—it's already shining for you. The white light is so clear, so alive with energy, that it makes you tingle all over, inside and out. It's as if every cell were being charged with energy.

Turn to look back at the tunnel behind you. Dark no more, it's now flooded with a rainbow of glowing light. You face forward once again, standing in the bright white light. Your energy centers have been switched on, and you're ready for a bright future.

When you do this visualization your subconscious will tell you which energy centers are weak and which are strong by how bright the lights are. Specific energy levels can be increased by picturing yourself putting in a higher-wattage bulb of that particular color.

Use this image whenever you need an energy boost and want to brighten up your life.

67

TOIL CHANGE

Have you been running in high gear up and down the hills and valleys of life? Toiling long hours? Like a car that has been revved too often and for too long, you could be suffering from sludge build-up. The sludge of sour thoughts. The gummy residue of disappointments and aggravations. Junk food gunk. If your internal engine is overdue for a "toil" change, here's how to do it.

Imagine that you're outdoors on a sunny day standing barefoot on grass, or earth, or sand. Feel the texture of the ground beneath your feet. Then focus on your body, starting with your feet and moving up to your head. Sense how the sludge inside you feels. Thick and heavy, it prevents you from running smoothly and efficiently. It gums up the works. The sludge makes you tired because you have to work that much harder to go the same distance or accomplish the same amount.

Looking down at your feet, you notice that the end of each toe is capped with a plug or a cork. You take a deep breath and exhale sharply to force energy down through your body and out your feet. The plugs or corks at the end of your feet pop out. Aided by gravity, black-brown gummy sludge starts draining out your toes. You watch as the oily slick spreads across the grass or earth, then soaks in and disappears.

Painlessly and effortlessly, the sludge empties first from your head and chest. As it drains from your chest it pulls sludge up from your fingertips, up your arms, and into your torso to drain. The sludge level gets lower and lower as it flows out of your body. Quarts of sludge drain effortlessly from your chest, abdomen, hips, pelvis, thighs, knees, and calves. Finally, the last pints in your feet flow out the ends of your toes and soak into the earth. Shake each foot to get out every last drop. Inside, you feel clean and clear; lighter in weight and lighter in attitude.

Push the plugs or corks back into the ends of your toes, and pull out the plug or cork on the very top of your head. Right by your side is a can of NuLife Oil—heavy or lightweight, depending on your needs. Punch two holes in the can; a large one for pouring and a small one for air. Then hold the can over your head and pour the new oil into the opening.

The NuLife oil flows in like nectar from the gods. Golden and sweet, it tickles deliciously as it trickles through your body. First your feet fill up with golden energy. Then your calves, knees, thighs, pelvis, hips, abdomen, chest, and, finally, your head fills with golden elixir. Every part of your body becomes lightly coated with clean new oil. You move fluidly. You think clearly. Everything works smoothly. You're full of clear, positive energy from head to toe.

Replace the plug or cork in the top of your head. Give it a firm push to keep in all that smooth, golden energy.

Don't let the pressures of life build up to the point where they gum up the works. Every six hundred hours or so of operation, give yourself a "toil" change. You'll be glad you did!

68

GIT OUTA DODGE

Sickness is a crime against health, with the criminal remaining on the premises. Don't allow illness to steal your health, ransack your body, vandalize your stamina, or hold you for ransom. Take action.

Imagine a Western-style sheriff with a silver star badge. He wears a white cowboy hat and sports a big, droopy mustache. You've alerted him to the fact that the notorious Illness Outlaw and his Illness Gang are hiding out on your land, plundering and looting. The sheriff has mounted a posse of determined, able-bodied men to ride with him over to your place.

Picture the landscape of your body: river veins, stream arteries, lake organs, rock bones, earth tissue, forests, hills, valleys, caves, canyons, etc. The sun casts light and shadow. Wind blows through canyons. Water flows. Somewhere in your bodyscape lurks the Illness Outlaw and his infamous gang.

It's early morning, the sun just creeping over the hills, when the sheriff and his posse ride up. You hear the pounding of the horses' hooves before you see them. You tell the sheriff where in your body you think the Illness Gang is hiding. He nods and says, "We'll get 'em for you, pardner." The sheriff has brought an extra horse for you. What color is it? Mount up and ride off alongside the sheriff, the posse behind you.

Even if you've never ridden, you sit tall in the saddle, controlling the horse like an old hand. The motion of the horse beneath you gives you a sense of power. As you ride, you feel more and more invigorated.

The sheriff has an unerring instinct for the whereabouts of the nefarious Illness Outlaw and his Illness Gang. He leads his posse right to their hideout, surprising the Illness Gang at high noon. Their hideout is barren, blackened with fires, and filthy, littered with waste.

Remaining safely behind a large rock, you watch as the sheriff and his posse ride into the gang's hideout, hooves thundering, guns drawn. The sheriff and his posse surround the Illness Outlaw and his ragtag Illness Gang, preventing anyone from escaping. Dismounting smoothly, never taking his gun off the Illness Outlaw, the sheriff says, "You lowdown, dirty varmints, you're finished in these-here parts."

The sheriff and his posse make the Illness outlaws return everything they stole from you: your health, your strength, your git-up-and-go. Then the sheriff and his posse make the Illness Gang clean up their mess, restoring your bodyscape to its original natural beauty.

The sheriff rounds up the Illness Outlaw and his Illness Gang, and runs them off your land, telling them never to show their ugly faces around these parts again. The Illness Outlaw and every last member of his Illness Gang git off your land faster than you can say, "I'm healthy." The land they pillaged is restored to complete health.

As you ride home alongside the sheriff, you sit tall in the saddle, glad to be healthy. As the ground flies by beneath your horse's hooves, you look at the grandeur of your bodyscape, feeling more and more feel powerful.

Reaching your homestead, you thank the sheriff and his posse for their help. The sheriff tips his hat to you and says, "Anytime. Anytime at all. We're here to serve and protect."

The honor of your health as been avenged, the crime rectified. You're alive with health, ready to live life to the fullest.

69
COLOR POWER

Do you want to make your life more colorful? Brighten up your gray matter? Feel in the pink? Here's how.

Travel in your mind to a place of beauty where the earth is at peace. A wide-open place from which you can see the curve of the earth against the horizon. A field. The seashore. A mountain peak. The desert at night when it's blooming.

Stand so that your feet are planted firmly on the ground. Admire the view, letting the sweep of it expand your mind. Your thoughts take wing, flying freely.

On the ground in front of you is a large crystal bowl. The bowl is empty but seems to be waiting to be filled. You put both hands around the sides of the bowl and lift it up. It's easy to hold, and light.

As you lift the bowl, something wondrous happens: you rise up off the ground. Into the sky you fly, the bowl in your hands. The bowl knows where to go, so you let it guide you. With grace and speed you glide across the earth, scooping up green, growing essence from the leaves of plants and trees, from fields of grass, from four-leaf clovers.

As soon as your bowl is full of vibrant green, you return to your place of peace and beauty, landing softly, feet first. A woman is waiting there for you. She may be a young maiden, a mature woman, or an elderly grandmother. She is the Earth Mother. In her cupped hands are rich green emeralds and peridots. They spill from her hands into your bowl, turning to glittering green gem dust that swirls and blends with the green of the growing earth.

Taking the bowl, she pours its contents over you. The green, growing energy flows over you and through you. It cleanses you. It empowers you. It sparks every cell with growth and health.

Again the bowl is empty and waiting. Again you lift the bowl and rise up into the sky. Soaring, you scoop blue from the sky, then dive to gather blue from the sea. Returning to your place of peace you find the Earth Mother; sapphires and turquoise fill her cupped hands. She pours them into your bowl of blue, then pours the blue over you. Your thoughts and emotions are cleansed and expanded.

Lifting again into the sky with the crystal bowl, you visit gardens and meadows filled with flowers, scooping up the lavender from violets, lilacs, petunias, orchids, and irises. Your bowl brimming with lavender, you land at your place of peace. The Earth Mother swirls amethyst dust into the bowl of lavender nectar and pours it over and through you. Your spiritual self pours through your mind and body, opening them. You feel loved.

Once more you fly through the sky carrying your bowl. Gliding gracefully across the earth, you gather the white from calla lilies, from white carnations, from white roses. You gather the white of snow, and the foamy crests of waves. You add a touch of gold from fields of wheat. Soaring, you scoop the bright white light of sunshine into your bowl, then return to your place of peace and beauty.

The Earth Mother stands there, cupped hands brimming with shimmering diamonds. Sunlight skips across the diamonds, sparking rainbow prisms. You hold out your bowl of light to the Earth Mother, and diamond dust, like a rainbow bridge, arcs into your waiting bowl, stirring the light already gathered there.

The Earth Mother takes the bowl from your hands and pours light over your head. The light spirals around and around your body, and down through your head to your feet. Every part of your body, mind, and spirit is enlivened. You feel in harmony with yourself and the world.

When you want to be cleansed and empowered, ground yourself on the earth, and let your spirit soar. Fill your bowl and your life with color power.

70

SKINNY DIPPING

Isn't it amazing how pants that come back from the cleaners seem to have shrunk? The old zipper just doesn't slide up easily—you have to pull and tug. Just in case you have a sneaking suspicion that it might be you and not the pants, here's a way to see a slimmer you—and so *be* a slimmer you.

Imagine that you're standing on the bank of your own private stream. Scattered along the banks of the meandering stream, and peeking out from the roots of trees, are bright spring flowers: daffodils, and tulips, and lilies-of-the-valley. Robins and sparrows sing in the trees, butterflies flutter and float nearby. A soft breeze stirs through your hair. The warmth of the sun sits comfortingly on your shoulders. You take off your shoes and wiggle your bare feet into the earth; blades of grass tickle your toes.

In front of you the stream shimmers in the sunlight, flowing gently from right to left. The rushing and tumbling sounds of the pure, gleaming water invite you in. Looking around to make sure that you're alone, you take off your clothes. At first you feel a little self-conscious, but as you undress a feeling of daring grabs you and you fling your clothes on the bank of the stream, letting them fall where they may.

Naked, you plunge into the stream. The water is refreshingly brisk, but comfortable. The stream is only about fifteen feet wide, and no deeper than you are tall, so you feel safe. You begin to swim, and play, and splash in the stream. The more you enjoy the water, the happier you become. You feel mighty fine about taking the plunge.

As you frolic in the water, you become aware that your body feels noticeably lighter. With pleasant surprise you realize that the water is softening your fat cells, and pounds of fat are literally melting away. From every area of your body that you want to be thinner, the fat just melts off and is swept away by the current. Well, well, you think, *this* is a fun and easy way to lose weight.

Look at the bank on which your old clothes are strewn about, and then look across to the opposite bank. A brand-new outfit is hanging from a tree branch, on a hanger, no less. Then something wonderful and unique happens. Even though you're still in the stream, you see the new and slimmer you climb up on the opposite bank. Seen from behind, your naked silhouette is definitely narrower. Your waist nips in, your buttocks are higher, and your thighs are more streamlined.

Take a moment to appreciate the improvements. Think about how much better you're going to feel being thinner. Think about how much more you're going to enjoy life. Thank the stream for carrying away those pounds, and give yourself a pat on the (now thinner) back for taking the plunge.

Then yet another wonderful and unique thing happens. You climb out of the stream, walk up behind your thinner self, and merge with your lighter and tighter self. Feel how much lighter your slimmer body feels. Jump up and down and skip around. Your new, thinner body feels delightfully carefree and comfortable.

Take your new clothes off the hanger; they're at least a size smaller than you were wearing before. Slip them on. Everything fastens and zips with ease around the new, slimmer you. Kick up your heels and do a happy little "skinny-dip" jig on the bank of your skinny stream. Whenever you want to lose weight, the stream is there waiting to melt those pounds away. *Olé!*

71
NOT A KNOT

You've been exerting yourself physically, mentally, or emotionally, and you're tied up in knots. Muscles, thoughts, and feelings have bunched up with tension and become tangled. It's a knotty problem, but visualization can help loosen those knots.

First, locate the areas of tension within you. Scan your body from your feet to your head, looking for both physical and non-physical tension. Check all potential trouble spots: feet, calves, knees, stomach, lower back, heart, shoulders, neck, jaw, temples, eyes, head, etc. In each area in which you sense tension, picture the tension as a tangle of rope tied up in knots. The more tension there is, the thicker the rope and the more numerous the knots. Mild tension might be seen as knotted string. The rope or string, and the area around it, will tend to look gray, because tension constricts vital circulation.

Maybe you've been on your feet all day, either literally, or figuratively in that you've had to "think on your feet." Picture your feet as two clumps of tangled, knotted rope. Or those ligaments in your knee are giving you trouble. Or you've been carrying a burden around, and your back is a bunch of knotted rope. Or you've had a lot on your mind, and your brain is a mass of knots.

Once you've located the major areas of tension, seeing them as tangled bunches of knotted rope or string, give all the knots, in all the areas, permission to release. As you focus on each area, say, "I release tension." Then visualize the knots coming undone easily and effortlessly. If you see yourself struggling to untie those blasted knots and fuming in frustration, you'll create tension instead of releasing it.

The knots loosen and fly apart smoothly and quickly. As soon as the knots are gone, the rope untangles and forms itself into a neat coil. Picture smooth circles within circles of rope lying neatly in your feet, your back, your head—wherever there was tension. Your body is getting shipshape. If the tension was mild, and you pictured string instead of rope, see a loosely wound but orderly ball of string.

As each knotty area becomes untangled, take a deep breath and let out a long sigh of relief. Vitality begins to circulate freely. The rope or string, and the area around it, turns healthy pink. Your feet feel so energized and flexible that you could dance the night away. Your knee feels strong and springy. Your back straightens proudly. Thoughts circulate freely through your mind. As muscles, thoughts, and feelings relax, they gain strength and flexibility.

You've released tension from top to bottom, back to front. Reaffirm relaxation in each area by picturing the neatly coiled strands of rope, or loosely wound balls of string.

When you want to check for tension, your subconscious will let you know which areas are tense by showing you pictures of knotted ropes. Simply release the knots, thereby releasing tension, until there's nary a knot anywhere.

72

HEALING HELPER

If any place in your body is tense, or dis-eased, or in pain, and you want to help heal it, this visualization's for you.

In the infinite and varied landscape of your mind, find a secluded, peaceful place where you feel strong and calm. A place of power that promotes healing.

It can be anywhere, in any time. It might be a room hung with richly brocaded tapestries in a magic castle. Or a cave with sparkling crystal stalactites growing from the domed roof. Perhaps a forest glen dappled with sunlight and carpeted with moss, or a penthouse with a spectacular view. Maybe a healing bay aboard the starship *Enterprise*, star-date now.

See, or sense, your place of power as clearly as possible. In the middle is a flat, comfortable area where you can lie down. You do so, streching lazily and wiggling your toes delightedly. Calm spreads through you like a soothing wave.

As you relax you become aware of a figure standing next to you. It might be a man, or a woman, young or old. She lays a hand tenderly on your shoulder, and you feel warmth radiating from her fingers. The helper's eyes shine with wisdom, and with a kind smile she asks where you have discomfort or pain.

You tell this helper, this healer, where it is that your body hurts, and ask for help. She nods, *yes.*

Your healing helper dips clean white cloths into a bowl of fragrant healing solution, and lays them gently on all the areas of your body that seek health—including a couple of trouble spots that you might not have mentioned, or weren't aware of.

The healing compresses rest softly on your body, exerting a gentle, but pleasant, tugging action. As the white cloths soak up tension and pain, they turn gray. Then charcoal gray. And finally black.

Your healing helper removes the blackened cloths, dropping

them into a white plastic garbage bag. The sense of peace you felt on lying down increases.

The figure then lovingly places a fresh set of soft white healing cloths on the same areas as before. These cloths also turn gray, and then black with physical and emotional toxins. Your healer removes them, dropping each cloth into the garbage.

A third set of cloths is placed tenderly on your body. Your healing helper waits a couple of minutes, but the cloths turn dove gray and no darker. All the tension, pain, and dis-ease in your body has been absorbed by the cloths. The healing is complete.

Your healer removes the last batch of cloths and drops them in the garbage bag, closing it with a knot. Again, she lays a warm hand tenderly on your shoulder. You thank her for helping to heal you. She smiles kindly, eyes shining, then giving your shoulder a gentle squeeze, she's gone, taking the white garbage bag to dispose of.

You feel noticeably better. Your body is relaxed and balanced. Vitality courses through your veins, bringing health to every cell. You feel renewed.

Whenever you want to help your body return to health, go to your place of peace and power and ask your healing helper to help heal you. Have healing cloths placed on your body as often as necessary to achieve the health you desire.

73

FIRE UP

Has the zip gone out of your life? Has that inner spark died? Are you dragging yourself through the days? Rekindle that inner fire with the following visualization.

Imagine a quiet, sandy beach at twilight. No one's there but you. Gentle waves lap against the shore. Facing the sea, you sit down to rest. The white sand cushions you as you watch the setting sun set the sky aflame.

As the sun sinks below the horizon, the air turns cool. Feeling chilly you look for wood to build a fire. Pieces of driftwood that the sea has sculpted into smooth, graceful shapes are scattered along the beach. But instead of being brown and gray, these pieces of wood are bright red. Red like cherries. Red like Santa Claus's suit. Red like a Valentine heart.

You gather up this trove of nature's art and stack the cherry-red wood in a loose pile. Build the pile well above the high-tide mark, so it's in no danger of being washed away. When the pile of red wood seems big enough, stuff bunches of dry seaweed into the crevices between the wood.

Fishing in your pocket, you find a packet of matches from your favorite restaurant. You strike the match, hearing the rasp of the head on the sandpaper, and the pouf as it bursts into flame. Hold the lit match to the seaweed. It catches immediately, and soon the fire is burning briskly. If necessary, add more pieces of wood until the red flames are as high as you are tall.

With your mind's eye, see the cheery, cherry-red flames leap against the darkening evening sky. With your mind's ear, hear the fire crackle and snap. Stand in front of the fire and let it warm you. Feel the fire's gentle warmth on your face. Turn around and feel the warmth of the fire on your back.

The heat seeps in through your clothes and warms your skin. Little by little the heat soaks through your skin and into your body until the very marrow of your bones feels warmed. You feel safe and at peace.

As you gaze into the fire you notice something strange. The red flames are leaping as brightly as ever, but the pieces of wood aren't turning to ash—they're not even charred. As you bend forward to get a closer look, you notice that the fire doesn't get hotter the closer you get—it remains at a comfortable temperature.

Curious, you reach your hand out toward the flames, closer and closer, and still the fire doesn't get hotter. A flickering flame brushes your hand, but doesn't burn it or even hurt it. In fact, the brush of the flame tickled pleasantly.

The energy radiating from the the red flames is like a magnet drawing you right into the fire. The red flames surround you vibrantly and lovingly. Your body begins to tingle with vitality and strength. Any place inside you that felt cold and lifeless is now enlivened with bright, warm energy. When you feel energized through and through, step out of the fire. You feel healthy and powerful; ready for action.

Whenever you feel droopy, in need of an energy boost, fire up by visualizing your ever-burning fire, red flames leaping against the night sky. Warm yourself in front of it; charge yourself within it!

74

THANKS BE TO BOD

Your body performs thousands of functions every minute of every hour of every day of every week of every month of every year of every decade of your life. Lungs breathe, blood flows, food digests, skin sweats, nerves synapse, muscles contract, hair grows, etc. Your body performs, but do you applaud?

Performers on stage tend to give better performances if they know that the audience is appreciative. The same is true for the performers inside your body. Each area of your body—whether it's playing a major or a minor role—performs on the stage of your life for your benefit. You'll be able to enjoy a better performance if you express your appreciation.

Begin by becoming aware of your body. Focus on your breathing: the gentle rush of air through your nose and down your throat; the warm breath flowing out through your mouth. Become quiet and still enough to feel the beat of your heart. Relax. Relax some more.

Now applaud your body. Do it from head to toe, or work up from your feet, or say thanks as different body areas come to mind. As you focus on each part's special contribution, show heartfelt appreciation. You might see yourself sitting in a box seat in your heart, applauding, whistling, and cheering as each body performer takes a bow. Or you could present each performer with a rose, or a gift. Maybe writing a thank-you note is more your style. You might want to say thank you the same way for every part of your body, or in different ways for different parts. Do what feels right for you.

Here are some body performances to applaud:

Thank you, skin, for protection.
Thank you, feet, for support.
Thank you, knees, for resilience.
Thank you, legs, for mobility.
Thank you, hips, for balance.
Thank you, bowels, for elimination.

Thank you, genitals, for pleasure.
Thank you, stomach, for digesting.
Thank you, heart, for love and life.
Thank you, blood, for energy.
Thank you, spine, for backing.
Thank you, arms, for reaching.
Thank you, hands, for touching.
Thank you, muscles, for motion.
Thank you, lungs, for breathing.
Thank you, neck, for flexibility.
Thank you, throat, for expression.
Thank you, mouth, for tasting.
Thank you, nose, for smelling.
Thank you, ears, for hearing.
Thank you, eyes, for seeing.
Thank you, mind, for thinking.

These are some of the parts that deserve applause—include whatever other thank you's you want. If parts of your body haven't been performing up to par due to fatigue or illness, be sure to give them an extra heartfelt thank you for all the times they performed beautifully—it will encourage their recovery.

Doing this visualization just before falling asleep will relax you, and you'll wake up feeling refreshed and energized. Say thanks on a regular basis; once a week or at least once a month. After all, your body gives thousands of lively performances every day. Thanks be to bod.

75

HANDLE WITH CARE

If this planetary body, earth, were a human body, it would be considered seriously ill. Much of the blood in its river veins and arteries is contaminated. Harmful surgery is being done on its rain-forest lungs, and the air it needs to breathe is polluted. It's having a heart attack and its internal organs are convulsing. Earth's tissue is becoming toxic with poisons. Its body is racked by chills and fever. A mineral deficiency is developing. It sheds acid tears of rain. And there are holes in the skin of its atmosphere. The earth needs intensive care and fast.

Imagine that you're a doctor who specializes in earth medicine. You might be a general practitioner who knows something about all areas, or a specialist with expertise in a specific area. Whether an earth G.P. or specialist, you care deeply about the patient. After all, you've known her since you were born, and you owe her your life.

Put on your doctor's coat. Is it green and blue like the earth? Or white? What insignia is on the breast pocket? Perhaps it's the embroidered outlines of the earth with a caduceus over it. Whatever your skill or inclination, do what you can to help heal the earth. Anything is possible, so let your imagination fly.

Talk to the earth as you would to a friend who was ill. Call her by name. Ask her where it hurts. Ask her where it hurts the most. Ask her what she would like you to do to help alleviate her pain and heal her. Care for the earth and comfort her as best you can.

Open your medicine bag; it might be an old-fashioned black one, or a futuristic molded silver metal case. Maybe you perform reconstructive surgery on the rain forests, implanting new trees. Or tenderly spread healing salve on the gaping wounds where trees have been cut down, or where there have been fires. The salve is rich in nutrients that promote growth.

Drop giant cleansing pills into oceans, lakes, and rivers. As the pills dissolve, they break up oil clots and break down contaminates. Then drop in vitamin pills to revitalize the sealife.

Cover the ground with a healing poultice that draws out toxins. When the poultice turns black with toxins, remove it and lay down another one. Change poultices until they stop turning black.

Graft a layer of healthy atmosphere-skin over the holes. See it take hold and heal; the holes becomes whole.

With your mind, fly at the speed of thought to fertile places, then carry the green essence of growth to infertile areas, reminding them how to grow. Sow gratitude. Shower the planet with love. Give the earth permission to grow through love instead of pain. Give the earth permission to be healthy.

Fly to the moon and look at the planet Earth. Picture her glowing with health. Her blue seas sparkle with clarity and life. She is green with growth, rich in vitality. Maybe you see a halo around the earth.

The earth's bounty sustains our bodies, and her majesty nourishes our spirits. Without a healthy earth, we cannot be healthy, so let's make it a healthy life for every body—both human and planetary!